LAURA WILHELM

STYLISH **SEWING**

35 PATTERNS AND INSTRUCTIONS FOR CLOTHES, TOYS AND HOME ACCESSORIES

LAURA WILHELM

STYLISH SEWING

35 PATTERNS AND INSTRUCTIONS FOR
CLOTHES, TOYS AND HOME ACCESSORIES

SEARCH PRESS

Do you sometimes think it would be fun to get your sewing machine out again, brush up on your skills and make some really stunning items from cheerful fabrics? Perhaps you just need a bit of a kick-start to become more creative and make some individual pieces?

In this book, you will find unique ideas for stylish bags and comfortable, loose-fitting pyjama bottoms suitable for the whole family, as well as chic cushion covers, charming ideas for your home, fashionable accessories and delightful gifts for your close friends and family.

Full-size patterns can be found on the pattern sheet and the instructions are explained step by step, so even complete beginners will find it easy to make the items shown in this book.

In fact, there are no limits to what you can do; you can even adapt the patterns and follow your own ideas with the help of our design sketches. The fabrics from the Free Spirit Collection can be combined in any way you wish. The contemporary, spotted patterns, traditional Vichy checks, romantic rose designs and classic stripes all work well together.

This book is guaranteed to make you want to start sewing!

Have fun!

Design sketches Fashionable ideas

... WOMEN'S SKIRTS ...

LITTLE SMOCK TOP

TIED AROUND
THE NECK

ELASTICATED
INSIDE

LARGE POCKET

...WOMENSWEAR/TOPS...

Design sketches Fashionable ideas

Reversible shoulder bags

Small shoulder bags

... LARGE AND SMALL BAGS ...

... BAGS IN ALL SHAPES AND SIZES ...

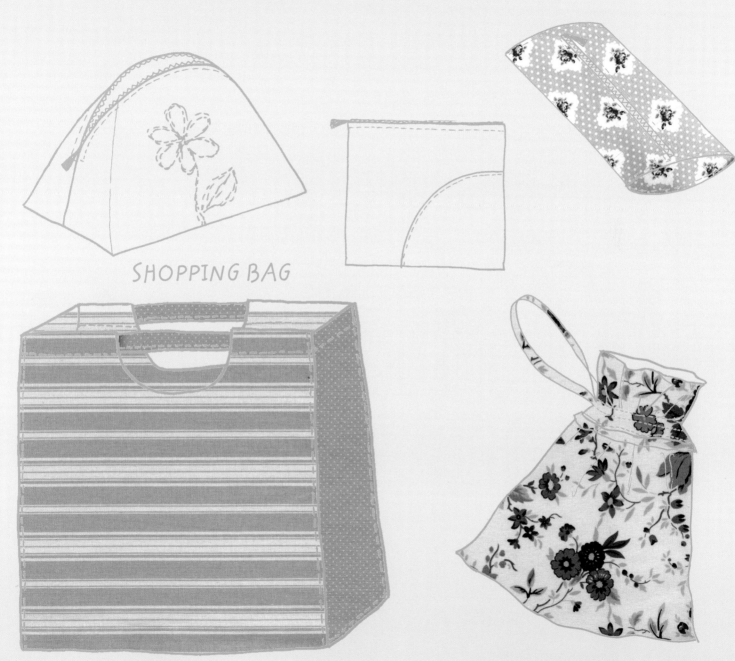

SHOPPING BAG

Design sketches Fashionable ideas

POCKETS IN
DIFFERENT FABRICS

... GIRLSWEAR ...

STRAWBERRY
APPLIQUÉ

SMOCKING WITH
SILK RIBBON

VELVET
RIBBON

... GIRLS' SKIRTS ...

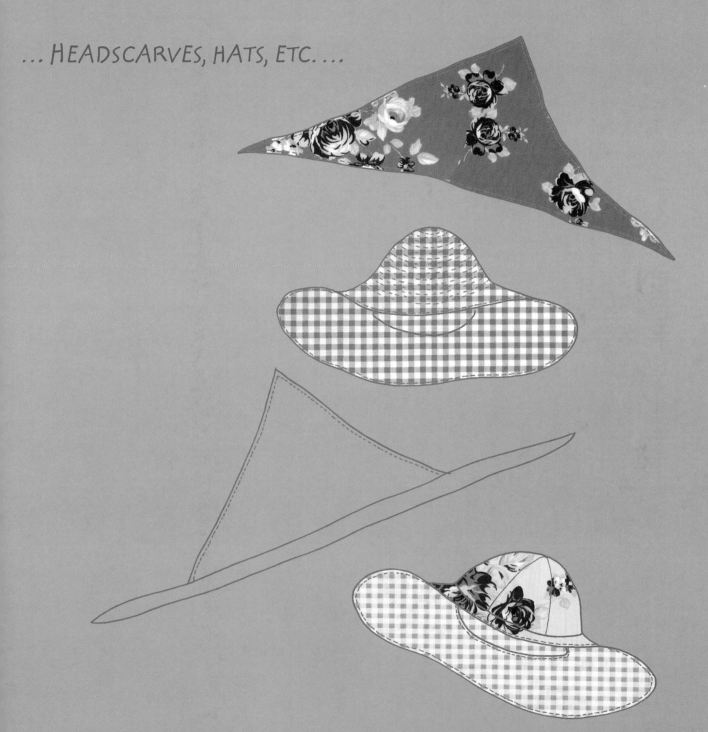

... HEADSCARVES, HATS, ETC. ...

... ORGANISING
AND STORING ...

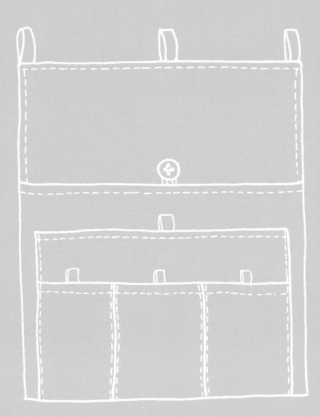

MOBILE PHONE
CASE WITH CLIP

MAKE-UP BAG

CAMERA CASE

... MOBILE PHONE, CAMERA, ETC. ...

...FLOOR CUSHIONS...

... LOOSE-FITTING PYJAMAS FOR ...

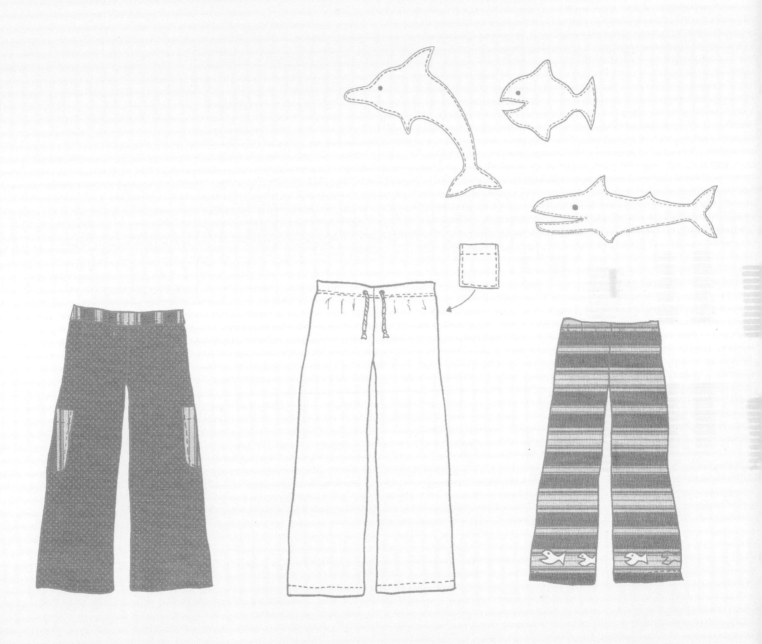

... THE WHOLE FAMILY ...

Design sketches Stylish living

SEWN-ON CIRCLES/MOTIFS

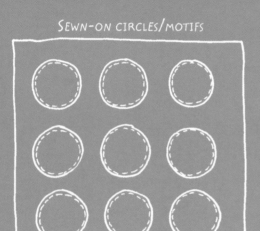

JOINED TOGETHER

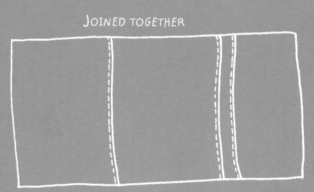

WITH APPLIQUÉ

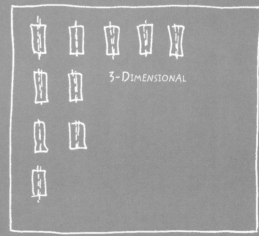

3-DIMENSIONAL

...CUSHION IDEAS...

...TOY TOWN ...

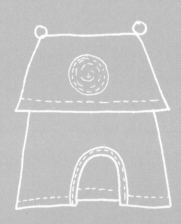

FASHIONABLE IDEAS

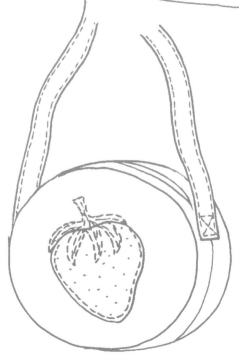

Patterned halterneck dress

LEVEL OF DIFFICULTY 2

SIZE
10/12, 14/16, 18/20

MATERIALS
Fabric A (QAH2400-SEA), 1.65m (65in) –
1.7m (67in) –1.75m (69in)

Fabric B (QVM1600-RAIN), 10cm (4in) for ties
at the back, remnant 30cm × 40cm
(11¾in × 15¾in) for pockets

Soft elastic, 2cm (¾in) wide, 35cm (13¾in) –
40cm (15¾in) – 45cm (17¾in)

Light blue sewing thread, e.g. Coats Cotton
number 50, colour 2336

PATTERN SHEET A (PINK)

When cutting out fabrics with large patterns, make sure the motifs are evenly spaced. Arrange the fold so that a striking or large motif sits centrally, rather than cutting into it or cutting it in half. Here, the large flower motif is arranged so that a whole flower sits at the bust line and three whole flowers run along the hem. The front and back pieces of the dress should also be equal, which may mean that you will need a bit more fabric to achieve an effect that looks balanced.

As the front and back pieces are almost identical, they have been drawn inside one another on the pattern sheet. The top edge of the back piece is marked.
The pattern on the sheet is 15cm (6in) longer than the model shown in the photo, so that you can adjust the length of the dress as you wish. Simply shorten the length at the hem. The amount of fabric has been worked out according to the long version.

SEAM AND HEM ALLOWANCES
For all seams and edges 1cm (½in) (top short edge of armhole facing has no seam allowance – see pattern diagram).
Bottom hem allowance 4cm (1½in).

SEWING INSTRUCTIONS
Cut out all the pieces according to the pattern. Neaten around all the edges of the front and back pieces as far as the hem, neaten all the facing pieces and the pockets using zigzag stitch.

TIES
Fold the neck tie in half along the length, wrong sides together, and sew, leaving one of the short sides open for turning out. Iron the seam allowances flat and turn the tie right side out. Use a blunt needle or a pencil to help push out the corners. Iron once more on the right side to obtain a sharp folded edge. Close up the open edge by hand.
Repeat the same process for the back ties, but neaten the openings for turning using zigzag stitch. They will be sewn into the side seams and will not therefore need to be closed up by hand.

ELASTIC BACK FACING
Iron the side seam allowances for the back facing over to the reverse by 1.2cm (½in) (the facing will be incorporated into the side seam later) and sew following the width of the sewing machine foot. Sew the top edge of the facing, right sides together, to the back piece and iron the seam allowances flat. Fold the facing inwards, turn up the seam allowance and tack. Sew the facing close to the edge.

	PATTERN PIECES		
1	Dress front	1 × fabric A on the fold line	
2	Dress back	1 × fabric A on the fold line	
3	Armhole facing front	1 × fabric A	
4	Drawstring channel facing front	1 × fabric A	
5	Elastic facing back	1 × fabric A	
6	Pockets	2 × fabric B	
	NOT ON THE PATTERN SHEET:		
7	Neck tie	1 × fabric A (cut 57cm × 10cm [22½in × 4in], 1cm [½in] seam allowance included)	
8	Ties at the back	2 × fabric B (cut 57cm × 12cm [22½in × 4¾in] each, 1cm [½in] seam allowance included)	

POCKETS

Iron the seam allowances over to the inside for the two rounded sides of the pockets, if necessary snipping into the seam allowances along the curves. Fold the pocket trims inside, turn up the seam allowances and sew 2cm (¾in) from the edge. Place the pockets on the front piece where marked and tack in place, so that the side seam allowances of the pockets are flush with the seam allowance of the front piece. Sew the rounded edges of the pockets twice (1mm [⅛in] and 7mm [⅜in] from the edge) and secure inside the side seam with a simple lockstitch.

ARMHOLE FRONT FACING

Tack the armhole facing to the edge of the armhole on the front piece, right sides together, and sew in place. Make sure that you place the facing piece 1cm (½in) below the top edge of the front piece, as there is no seam allowance on the top short edge as shown on the pattern. Iron the seam allowances flat, fold the armhole facings outwards and lay the seam allowances towards the front piece.

DRAWSTRING CHANNEL FRONT FACING

Tack the top edge of the facing, right sides together, to the top edge of the front piece, making sure again that the seam allowances at the armhole for the front piece are lying towards the centre front. The side seam allowances for the facing for the drawstring channel are not turned up, leaving a 1cm (½in) excess. Sew in place, incorporating the ironed-over seam allowances of the front piece. Iron the seam allowances flat. Fold the facing up. Lay the seam allowances towards the front piece.

Lay the armhole facing towards the inside over the seam allowance for the front piece and the facing for the drawstring channel. At the same time, the side seam allowance for the facing for the drawstring channel is also turned inwards. Iron the armhole very carefully, snipping the seam allowances if necessary, and tack in place. Topstitch the armhole seam starting at the side seam, following the width of the sewing machine foot, and continuing up over the drawstring channel. The seam allowance for the drawstring channel is sewn in at the same time. Lay the facing for the drawstring channel inwards, turn up the seam allowance and sew in place 2.5cm (1in) from the top edge.

Place the front and back pieces right sides together and tack. Place the ties on the markings so that when the sides are sewn up they are incorporated at the same time.

Close up the side seams, iron the seam allowances flat and turn the dress right side out. Thread through the neck tie.

Thread the elastic through the channel and secure to one side of the side seam beneath the seam. Try on and adjust the length of the elastic, then sew into the side seam on the other side in the same way.

Pretty girls' dress
Details on page 30

Pretty girls' dress

LEVEL OF DIFFICULTY 3

HEIGHT
1.1m (43¼in) – 1.22m (48in) – 1.34m (52¾in)

MATERIALS
Fabric A (QTW1800-PINK), 1.55m (61in) – 1.6m (63in) – 1.65m (65in)

Fabric B (QVM1800-GERAN), 15cm × 30cm (6in × 11¾in) for strawberry appliqué

Velvet or satin ribbon, in matching colour, 1cm (½in), 1.2m (47¼in) – 1.25m (49¼in) – 1.3m (51¼in)

Double-sided adhesive web, e.g. Vliesofix, 15cm × 30cm (6in × 11¾in) for the strawberry appliqué

Fleece interfacing for button tape trim

Pink sewing thread, e.g. Coats Cotton number 50, colour 2511

Natural-coloured embroidery yarn, e.g. Coats Creative number 16, colour 1418

Three to five buttons, in matching colour

PATTERN SHEET A (DARK GREEN)

The trims for the button tape are cut out and reinforced with interfacing as shown on the pattern. The individual buttonholes marked relate to the three buttons with 1.5cm (⅝in) diameter and for the dress sizes 1.22m/1.34m. For more buttons or for the 1.1m pattern size, the buttonholes will need to be positioned and adjusted accordingly.

SEAM AND HEM ALLOWANCES
For all seams and edges 1cm (½in).
No seam allowance for the inner edges of the facing.
Bottom hem allowance 4cm (1½in).
No hem allowance for strawberry motifs.

SEWING INSTRUCTIONS
Cut all the pieces from fabric A according to the pattern.
Reinforce the button tape trim on the wrong side with fleece interfacing, avoiding the seam allowances. Neaten the raw edges of the front and back pieces to as far as the hem and all around the other pieces using zigzag stitch.

Iron on adhesive web to fabric piece B, draw on the strawberry motif twice (mirror images) and cut out. Remove the backing paper from the adhesive web and iron the strawberries on to the front piece of the dress according to the placement instructions.
Stitch around the strawberries and embroider the strawberry stalks by machine: transfer the shape of the stalks to the fabric following the placement instructions. Select a stronger sewing needle (90–100) and use the natural-coloured embroidery yarn as a top thread. Check the size of the stitch on a remnant of fabric, stitch length approximately 3.5mm (¼in); if necessary, relax the top thread tension a little. Sew twice roughly around the outlines of the offset strawberries using the natural-coloured embroidery yarn, at the same time sewing the offset stalk once or twice too.
Change the sewing needle and thread again.
Place the front and back pieces right sides together, sew the shoulder seams and iron the seam allowances flat.
Iron the outside seam allowances of the trims for the rear button tape to the wrong side and tack in place. Turn the trims outwards, right sides together, and pin in place at the neckline. Stitch the trims along the lower edges as far as the back centre seam. Snip diagonally into the seam allowances at the corners of the ends of the seams. Sew together the inner facing for the back piece with the inner facing for the front piece at the shoulder seams. Iron the seams flat.
Tack the facing right sides together to the neckline with the shoulder seams together. Pin the seam allowance of the open ends of the rear neckline facing 1cm (½in) between the turned-up and pinned trims of the button tape.

1	Dress front	1 × fabric A on the fold line
2	Dress back	2 × fabric A
3	Neckline inner front facing	1 × fabric A on the fold line
4	Neckline inner back facing	2 × fabric A
5	Armhole inner front facing	2 × fabric A
6	Armhole inner back facing	2 × fabric A
7	Strawberry motif with placement instructions	2 × fabric B
	NOT ON THE PATTERN SHEET:	
4	Draw cord trim	1 × (cut 72cm [28¼in] – 76cm [30in] – 80cm [31½in] × 3.5cm [1½in], 1cm [½in] seam allowance included)

PATTERN PIECES AND MOTIFS

Sew around the top edge of the trims (seam allowance remains folded over and is incorporated) and the inner facing. Trim the seam allowances and snip at the curves if necessary. Turn the trims and the inner facing inside and iron. Topstitch around the neckline, including the button tape on the right side, following the width of the sewing machine foot. Sew the button tape in place close to the edge. Sew the centre back seam and side seams and iron the seam allowances flat. Sew together the inner facing around the armhole at the shoulder and side seams. Iron the seam allowances flat.

Tack the facings, right sides together, to the armholes, with the shoulder and side seams together. Sew around the facings, turn inside and iron. Sew in place from the right side, following the width of the sewing machine foot.

Iron under the narrow sides of the draw cord trim 1cm (½in) towards the inside, turn up and sew. Iron the long edges to the reverse of the fabric by 1cm (½in). Tack the trim to the dress as shown and sew close to the edge along the long edges. Make the buttonholes on the left back piece either as shown or adjusted as required. Sew on the buttons.

Pull the velvet or satin ribbon through the drawstring channel. Work out the length of the ties and shorten if necessary. Turn up the raw edges of the ribbons twice and finish off by hand.

Baby clothes

SEAM AND HEM ALLOWANCES

For all seams and edges 1cm (½in).
Bottom of gathered trim 2cm (¾in).

SEWING INSTRUCTIONS

Cut out all the pieces according to the pattern. Tack the front piece to the back piece right sides together. Sew the shoulder and side seams. Neaten together the seam allowances using zigzag stitch. Sew the gathered trim along the short edges, right sides together. Neaten the seam allowance together using zigzag stitch.

Fold the bottom edge of the gathered trim under by 2cm (¾in), turn up 7mm (⅜in) and sew close to the edge.

Sew rows of running stitch along the top edge of the trim (see instructions on page 111) and gather up to fit the length of the bottom edge of the dress. Tack the gathered trim, right sides together, to the edge of the dress and sew in place. The seam on the gathered trim can be matched up with either a side seam or the centre back. Neaten the seam allowances together using zigzag stitch. Press upwards.

Cut into the front piece of the dress at the centre front as far as the marking for the end of the slit. Iron the seam allowances to the inside (the wrong side). The seam allowances run at an angle away to the end of the slit. Sew the seam allowances from the right side using zigzag stitch (stitch width approximately 3–4mm [¼in], stitch length approximately 2–3mm [⅛in]), so that the edge of the seam allowance is completely incorporated. Repeat the same process for the seam allowances around the armholes.
This method may be a little unconventional, but it is very easy and effective to use. The zigzag stitch, which is normally only used for neatening, gives a very decorative appearance here.

If you are having difficulty with this method, you can use a matching bias binding instead.

Sew on the fabric rose by hand at the base of the slit.

PATTERN PIECES			
	1	Front piece of dress	1 × fabric A on the fold line
	2	Back piece of dress	1 × fabric A on the fold line
		NOT ON THE PATTERN SHEET:	
	3	Gathered trim	1 × fabric A (cut out 1.15m × 13cm [45¼in × 5in], seam allowance of 1cm [½in] included)

LEVEL OF DIFFICULTY 2

HEIGHT
74cm (29¼in) – 86cm (33¾in)

MATERIALS
Fabric A (QVM1700-ROSE),
60cm (23½in)

Pink sewing thread, e.g. Coats
Cotton number 50,
colour 2511

Small fabric rose
for decoration

PATTERN SHEET A (RED)

Floaty women's skirt

When cutting out fabric with large patterns, make sure that the motifs are evenly spaced. Arrange the fabric fold line so that a striking or large motif is centred and looks right once the piece has been cut out. In this example, the large flowers are cut exactly in half along the top edge and then appear twice below along the run of the skirt. The front and back pieces of the skirt should also be the same. You may therefore need more fabric to achieve a better, more balanced look to the pattern.

SEAM AND HEM ALLOWANCES
For all seams and edges 1cm (½in).

SEWING INSTRUCTIONS
Cut out all the pieces according to the pattern. Mark the side lines for the pleats and the end of the slit for the zip fastener. Neaten the side seams using zigzag stitch.

Fold the front piece of the skirt (with the right side of the fabric inside), so that the pleat lines meet. Sew down the pleat lines for 5cm (2in) as shown on the pattern. Iron the depth of the pleat flat and sew or tack inside the seam allowances. Repeat the same process for the pleats on the back piece of the skirt.

Lay the front and back pieces of the skirt right sides together, tack the side seams and sew. Make sure that the left side seam is sewn only from the end of the slit to the bottom. Iron the seam allowances flat, leaving the slit still tacked. Tack the zip fastener beneath the edges of the slit, leaving the teeth hidden. Sew on the zip fastener using the zipper foot. Iron interfacing on to the pieces for the waistband.

Lay the front waistband on to the back waistband right sides together and sew the right side seam. Iron the seam allowances flat. Neaten the bottom edge of the waistband using zigzag stitch.

Back the waistband to the top edge of the skirt, right sides together, with the closed side seam meeting up with the closed waistband seam. Turn up the seam allowances of the side waistband edges, wrong sides together. Sew the waistband in place. Remove the tacking threads. Position the waistband upwards and iron the seam allowances into the waistband. Iron the waistband under towards the inside and tack. Topstitch the top edge of the skirt from the right side following the width of the sewing machine foot.

Sew the edges of the waistband by hand along the tapes of the zip fastener.

Tack the front hem border to the back hem border, right sides together, and sew the side seams. Iron the seam allowances flat. Turn the skirt inside out. Tack the right side of the border to the wrong side of the bottom edge of the skirt and sew in place. Turn the skirt out. Iron the border under to the right side of the skirt. Turn the seam allowance inwards at the top edge of the border. Sew close to the edge of the border.

PATTERN PIECES			
	1	Front piece of skirt	1 × fabric A on the fold line
	2	Back piece of skirt	1 × fabric A on the fold line
	3	Front hem border	1 × fabric B on the fold line
	4	Back hem border	1 × fabric B on the fold line
	5	Front waistband	1 × fabric B on the fold line
	6	Back waistband	1 × fabric B on the fold line
			reinforce with interfacing on the wrong side

LEVEL OF DIFFICULTY 2

SIZE
10/12, 14/16, 18/20

MATERIALS
Fabric A (QAH2400-ZINNI),
1.35m (53¼in)

Fabric B (QTW1800-PINK),
80cm (31½in) cut on the bias
as here in checks (40cm
[15¾in] cut on the grain)

7in fastener, 16cm (6¼in),
e.g. Opti S40, colour 749

Light interfacing fabric for
the front and back waistband

Pink sewing thread, e.g.
Coats Cotton number 50,
colour 2511

**PATTERN SHEET A + B
(ORANGE)**

LEVEL OF DIFFICULTY 2

HEIGHT
98cm (38½in)/1.04m (41in),
1.16m (45¾in)/1.22m (48in),
1.34m (52¾in)/1.4m (55in)

MATERIALS
Fabric A (QVM1800-GERAN),
40cm (15¾in) – 50cm
(19¾in) – 60cm (23½in)

Fabric B (QTW1700-GRAPE),
35cm (13¾in) – 40cm
(15¾in) – 45cm (17¾in)

Velvet or satin ribbon, 1cm
(½in), in matching colour,
1.25m (49¼in) – 1.3m
(51¼in) – 1.35m (53¼in)

Soft elastic, 1.5cm (⅝in)
wide, 50cm (19¾in) – 55cm
(21¾in) – 60cm (23½in)

Red sewing thread, e.g.
Coats Cotton number 50,
colour 7810

Two decorative buttons
for the pockets in a
matching colour

**PATTERN SHEET A
(LILAC)**

Floaty girls' skirt

The front and back pieces of the skirt pattern are cut the same, which is why you will find just one pattern piece on the pattern sheet.

SEAM AND HEM ALLOWANCES
For all seams and edges 1cm (½in).
Hemline 3cm (1¼in).

SEWING INSTRUCTIONS
Cut out all the pieces according to the pattern. Sew gathering threads (see page 111) along the pockets in the area shown directly on the edge and lightly gather. Fold the pocket trims inwards, turn up the seam allowances and sew in place 2cm (¾in) from the edge. Cut two velvet ribbons, each 11cm (4¼in) long, for the pockets.

Tack the velvet ribbons 2cm (¾in) away from the edge on to the seam of the trim, so that it is hidden. Stitch the velvet ribbons close to the edge on both sides. Iron under the seam allowances for the pockets. Place the pockets on the front skirt piece: tack the pockets on to the skirt piece 7cm (2¾in) – 8cm (3¼in) – 8.5cm (3¼in) parallel with the centre front and 3cm (1¼in) – 5cm (2in) – 7cm (2¾in) away from the bottom edge and sew close to the edge.

Sew gathering threads along the top edge of the hem border and gather up to fit the length of the bottom edge of the skirt.

Tack and sew the hem border to the skirt pieces, right sides together. Neaten the seam allowances together using zigzag stitch, position upwards and iron. Sew one side seam and neaten the seam edges together using zigzag stitch.

Tack the velvet ribbon flush with the dividing seam on to the side of the skirt pieces (still allowing a 1cm [½in] seam allowance) and sew both close to the edge. Sew and neaten the other side seam, incorporating the velvet ribbon into the seam allowance at the same time.

Fold the hem seam allowance under by 3cm (1¼in), turn up by 1cm (½in) and sew 2cm (¾in) from the edge. Sew together the skirt waistband along the short side, right sides together, and neaten the seam allowances together using zigzag stitch.

Sew the skirt waistband to the skirt, right sides together, placing the seam of the waistband exactly on top of the left side seam. Neaten the seam allowances together using zigzag stitch and iron into the skirt waistband. Fold the skirt waistband inwards at the fold line, turn up the seam allowance and tack in place. Sew into the seam from the right side, leaving a 4cm (1½in) opening for the elastic. Work out the width of the elastic channel, cut the elastic with a 6cm (2¼in) seam allowance and thread through. Sew the elastic together with a 3cm (1¼in) overlap either by hand or using the machine. Close up the hole for threading. Sew decorative buttons on to the pockets by hand.

PATTERN PIECES			
	1	Front piece of skirt	1 × fabric A on the fold line
	2	Back piece of skirt	1 × fabric A on the fold line
	3	Hem border	2 × fabric B on the fold line
	4	Skirt waistband attached	1 × fabric B on the fold line
	5	Pockets	2 × fabric B

Reversible summer hat

LEVEL OF DIFFICULTY 2

SIZE
Up to a head circumference of 56cm (22in)

MATERIALS
Fabric A (QTW2200-BLUSH), 40cm (15¾in)

Fabric B (QTW1800-PINK), 40cm (15¾in)

Fleece interfacing, thickness 40cm (15¾in)

White sewing thread, e.g. Coats Cotton number 50, colour 2716

PATTERN SHEET A (LIGHT GREEN)

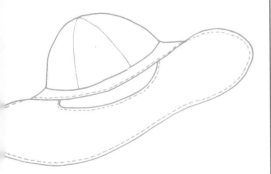

SEAM ALLOWANCES
Curved side head pieces without seam allowance (7mm [⅜in] already included).
For all other pattern edges 1cm (½in).

Even if it does take a little longer, it is worth sewing together the six parts of the hat from a piece of test fabric to check the width. The seam allowance at the sides of 7mm (⅜in) has already been included in the pattern. If, for example, you stitch 8mm (⅜in) away from the edge all around, the circumference will be reduced by 1.2cm (½in), and the circumference will be enlarged by 1.2cm (½in) if you sew just 6mm (¼in) from the edge. Any change in circumference must be taken into account (enlarged or reduced) at the top edge of the hat brim.

SEWING INSTRUCTIONS
Cut out the pieces according to the pattern. Reinforce all the pieces from fabric A with the fleece interfacing. Sew together the six hat pieces from fabric A one after the other and right sides together, starting at the bottom, up to the upper centre (according to the pattern, 7mm [⅜in] from the edge or as desired on the test piece). Carefully iron each of the seam allowances flat.

Tack and sew together both pieces of the hat brim, right sides together. Iron the seam allowances flat. Repeat the same process for the six hat pieces from fabric B and the hat brim B.
Tack hat brim A to hat brim B, right sides together. Sew the outer brim seam, iron the seam allowances flat and turn right side out.
Pin hat piece B into hat piece A, wrong sides together, making sure that the seam allowances line up with one another. Tack or sew together the hat pieces at the bottom edge inside the seam allowances.
Tack the brim to the hat pieces, so that brim fabric A lies right sides together with hat piece A. Sew brim A along the bottom edge of hat piece A + B. Fold in the seam allowances for brim B and tack in place, so that they can later be sewn close to the edge from the top side along the seam. Starting from the outer edge of the brim, the brim can then be decorated with lines of stitching as desired and reinforced.
If the inside of the brim proves to be too big, you can run some gathering stitches through it and lightly gather to make it the correct width.

PATTERN PIECES			
	1	Hat piece, outside	6 × fabric A
			complete with Vlieseline reinforcing
		Hat piece, inside	6 × fabric B
	2	Brim, outside	2 × fabric A
			complete with Vlieseline reinforcing
		Brim, inside	2 × fabric B

Summary strawberry bag

SEAM ALLOWANCES

1cm (½in) seam allowances included.
Reinforce all pieces with fleece interfacing; for the shoulder strap exclude the seam allowances.

SEWING INSTRUCTIONS

Cut out all the pieces according to the instructions and reinforce with fleece interfacing as instructed. Iron adhesive web on to fabric piece C, draw on the mirror image of the strawberry motif and cut out. Remove the backing paper from the adhesive web and iron the strawberries on to the centre of the two outer bag circles.

Place the inner bag circles against the outer bag circles, wrong sides together, and tack in place. They will be held in place by sewing around the edge of the strawberries.

Sew around the strawberries and embroider the stalks by machine: transfer the outline of the stalks to the fabric following the placement instructions. Select a larger sewing machine needle (90–100) and insert the natural-coloured embroidery yarn as the top thread. Check the size of the stitch on a remnant of fabric, stitch length approximately 3.5mm (⅛in). If necessary, relax the top thread tension a little.

Now sew roughly around the outlines of the offset strawberries twice using the natural-coloured embroidery yarn, at the same time sewing the offset stalks once or twice too.
Change the sewing needle and thread again.

Place the side pieces on top of one another, right sides together, and tack in place. Sew the pieces together exactly in the middle along the length, leaving 20cm (7¾in) open in the centre. Secure the ends of the seams well. Fold down the side pieces and iron flat, so that the right sides of the fabric and the 20cm (7¾in) bag opening can be seen on both sides. Sew the side piece together at the short ends, right sides together. Neaten the seam allowances together using zigzag stitch.

Tack and sew the side piece to a bag piece, right sides together (the right side here is the side with the strawberry appliqué). Make sure that the stalk of the strawberry is pointing upwards towards the opening of the bag. The sewing will be most accurate when the circle is lying flat against the sewing machine table, wrong side down, and the side piece is on top. This is the best way to ensure that the pieces stay flat when sewn together.

Turn the bag inside out and sew the other side of the side piece to the other bag circle. Neaten the seam allowances together all around using a narrow zigzag stitch.

Iron under the seam allowances for the shoulder strap to the wrong side. Fold the strap along the length and iron. All the edges should be lying neatly on top of one another with the seam allowances turned in.
Sew the edges close to the edge. Tack 4cm (1½in) at each end of the strap directly to the ends of the opening for the bag and sew to the side piece.

If you would like to attach a fastening to the bag opening, then after sewing together the side pieces, sew on a zip fastener in a matching colour (length 20cm [7¾in]). Tack the zip fastener into the opening, making sure the teeth remain hidden. Sew the zip fastener in place from the right side using the zipper foot.

You can enlarge or reduce the measurements for the bag as you wish: set the size of the circle and work out the right length for the side piece as follows: (circle diameter without seam allowance) × 3.14 = length of side piece without seam allowance. You can adjust the width of the side piece according to the size of the bag.

Also, instead of the shoulder strap, you can attach two small handles or finished bag handles (e.g. wooden rings).

PATTERN PIECES AND MOTIFS				
	4	Strawberry appliqué	See strawberry dress on page 29 – reduced by 90%	2 × fabric C
		NOT ON THE PATTERN SHEET:		
	1a	Outer bag	Circle with 23cm (9in) diameter	2 × fabric A
	1b	Inner bag	Circle with 23cm (9in) diameter	2 × fabric A
	2	Shoulder strap	7cm × 1.12m (2¾in × 44in)	1 × fabric A
	3	Side piece	8cm × 68cm (3¼in × 26¾in)	2 × fabric B

LEVEL OF DIFFICULTY 2

SIZE
Diameter 21cm (8¼in)
Depth of bag 6cm (2¼in)

MATERIALS
Fabric A (QTW1800-PINK),
35cm (13¾in)

Fabric B (QVM1300-MILK),
20cm (7¾in)

Fabric C (QVM1800-GERAN),
15cm × 30cm (6in × 11¾in)
for strawberry appliqué

Firm, iron-on fleece
interfacing, for all
pattern pieces

Double-sided adhesive web,
e.g. Vliesofix, 15cm × 30cm
(6in × 11¾in) for
strawberries

Pink sewing thread, e.g.
Coats Cotton number 50,
colour 2511

Natural-coloured embroidery
yarn, e.g. Coats Creative,
colour 1418

PATTERN SHEET A
(LIGHT LILAC)

Strawberry and dolphin **T-shirts**

Beautiful appliqué can be made quickly and easily from remnants of fabric. If necessary, they can even be used to cover holes or marks and can transform off-the-peg T-shirts into something quite unique and individual.
The process is described on page 40 for the strawberry bag.

Simple cotton shopping bags, plain pyjamas and tablecloths can also be turned into personalised gifts using appliqué motifs.

N.B.
For knitted fabrics (single jersey, sweatshirt fabric and stretchable fabrics), you must use a special sewing machine needle with a rounded tip or a jersey needle. Normal needles will damage the stitches and leave big holes, and the colours may run after the first wash.
For thinner T-shirt fabrics, it is advisable to reinforce the area for the appliqué on the wrong side with fleece interfacing before sewing.

Floral headscarf

LEVEL OF DIFFICULTY 1

SIZE
Suitable for all sizes

MATERIALS
Fabric A (QVM1300-MILK), approximately 40cm × 80cm (15¾in × 31½in)

Fabric B (QVM1800-MILK), approximately 10cm × 1m (4in × 39¼in)

Natural-coloured sewing thread, e.g. Coats Cotton number 50, colour 1418

PATTERN SHEET A (LIGHT BLUE)

PATTERN PIECES			
1	Headscarf	1 × fabric A on the fold line
2	Tie trim, sewn on	1 × fabric B on the fold line

SEAM ALLOWANCES
For all seams 1cm (½in).

SEWING INSTRUCTIONS

Cut out both pieces according to the pattern.
Turn up the two identical sides of the headscarf twice (1cm [½in] each) and topstitch close to the edge. Trim the excess seam edge.
Fold the tie trim in half, right sides together, at the fold line shown and iron. Iron the seam allowances upwards. Open up again.
Tack the tie trim, right sides together, centred along the length of the headscarf and sew in place.

Shoulder bag with appliqué

Use the relatively deep piece that is left over after the handles have been cut out to make a mini matching dolls' bag. To do this, simply reduce the pattern piece for the bag by forty-five per cent.

For a girls' bag reduce the pattern by seventy per cent.

SEAM AND HEM ALLOWANCES

For all seams and edges 1cm (½in).

SEWING INSTRUCTIONS

Cut out all the pieces according to the pattern and neaten around the edges using zigzag stitch.

Iron the heart motif on to the centre of the shirt pocket using adhesive web. When marking the centre, remember that another 4cm (1½in) will be turned under at the top for the trim and there will be an additional 1cm (½in) seam allowance turned up at the bottom.

Sew around the shape of the heart by machine: insert a larger sewing needle (90–100) and change the top thread for red embroidery yarn. Check the size of the stitch on a remnant of fabric, stitch length approximately 3.5mm (¼in). If necessary, relax the top thread tension a little. Sew roughly over the shape of the heart a few times with the red embroidery yarn. Change the sewing needle and thread again.

Iron the seam allowances of the shirt pocket inwards. Fold the pocket trim inwards (a total of 4cm [1½in] including the seam allowance), turn up the seam allowances and sew in place 3cm (1¼in) from the edge. Tack the shirt pocket centred on to a bag piece A and sew close to the edge.

Apply another motif to the inside pocket to make the bag look different when turned the other way out. Alternatively, apply a motif after sewing the bag pieces inside one another, then the shape of the stitching will also appear on the other side. Make sure you use a matching yarn for the lower machine thread.

Place the bag pieces in fabric A right sides together and tack. Sew a continuous side and base seam, starting at one tip of the cut-out handles right through to the other tip. Iron the seam allowances flat. Repeat the same process for the bag pieces in fabric B.

Pull bag piece B into bag piece A, right sides together, with the side seams meeting. Sew outer bag A to inner bag B, starting at the centre of a bag and sewing all the way around. Just before the end, leave 8cm (3¼in) open for turning. Turn the bag the right side out and iron. Close up the opening for turning by hand.

1 Bag	2 × fabric A on the fold line, 2 × fabric B on the fold line
2 Heart motif	1 × fabric C
NOT ON THE PATTERN SHEET:	
3 Shirt pocket with appliqué finished pocket 19cm × 16cm (7½in × 6¼in)	1 × fabric D (cut 24cm × 18cm [9½in × 7in], seam allowance 1cm [½in] and trim 3cm [1¼in] included)

PATTERN PIECES AND MOTIFS

LEVEL OF DIFFICULTY 2

SIZE
32cm × 45cm (12½in × 17¾in)
(without handle)

MATERIALS
Fabric A (QTW2000-GREEN),
95cm (37½in)

Fabric B (QTW1800-GREEN),
95cm (37½in)

Fabric C (QTW2100-FOX),
remnant for heart appliqué

Fabric D (QTW1800-PINK),
remnant 20cm × 25cm (7¾in
× 9¾in) for patch pocket

Double-sided adhesive web,
e.g. Vliesofix, 15cm × 12cm
(6in × 4¾in) for
heart appliqué

White sewing thread, e.g.
Coats Cotton number 50,
colour 2716

Red embroidery yarn, e.g.
Coats Creative number 16,
colour 7810

**PATTERN SHEET A
(DARK BLUE
AND TURQUOISE)**

Patterned bag set

LEVEL OF DIFFICULTY 2

SIZE

Zip-fastened bag 18cm × 24cm (7in × 9½in)
Mobile phone case 9cm × 15cm (3½in × 6in)

MATERIALS

ZIP-FASTENED BAG

Fabric A (QAH2400-SEA), 50cm × 32cm
(19¾in × 12½in)

Fabric B (QVM1600-RAIN), 50cm × 32cm
(19¾in × 12½in)

Firm, iron-on interfacing, 50cm × 32cm
(19¾in × 12½in) for outer pocket

Zip fastener, 30cm (11¾in), e.g. Opti S40,
colour 298

Light blue sewing thread, e.g. Coats Cotton
number 50, colour 2336

Beads, small crystals, small piece of felt,
narrow satin ribbon for decoration

MOBILE PHONE CASE

Fabric A (QAH2400-SEA), see table for
measurements

Fabric B (QVM1600-RAIN), see table for
measurements

Iron-on, one-sided volume fleece, see table
for measurements

Hook-and-loop fastening, 2cm (¾in) wide,
4cm (1½in)

Small ribbons, 1cm (½in) wide, 6cm (2¼in)

White sewing thread, e.g. Coats Cotton
number 50, colour 2716

Karabiner hook, 5cm (2in) (DIY store or
craft shop)

Beads, small crystals, mother-of-pearl
buttons, felt for decoration

DIAGRAM

Pattern sheet A

PATTERN SHEET A (BLACK)

Zip-fastened bag

SEAM ALLOWANCES

Iron the interfacing on to fabric A before cutting
and then cut out with the seam allowance.

SEWING INSTRUCTIONS

Cut out all the pieces according to the instructions
and reinforce with interfacing as instructed.
Tack the outer bag to the inner bag, right sides
facing, and sew together, leaving an opening for
turning on one side of approximately 7cm (2¾in).
Iron the seam allowances flat. Turn the piece right
side out and iron again. Close up the opening for
turning by hand.
Fold up the bag (fabric A is inside) and tack. Sew
the side seams as far as the marking for the zip
fastener. Iron the seam allowances flat.

SEW DARTS IN THE BASE

Place the corners at the base of the bag in such a
way that the side seam runs along the centre of
the base in the direction of the tips of the corners.
Sew the darts at right angles to the side seam
3.5cm (1½in) from the tip of the corner (see
instructions on page 109).

Fold the corner upwards towards the side seam
and secure with a few stitches by hand. Turn the
bag right side out.
Tack the zip fastener into the opening, with the
teeth remaining hidden. Sew the zip fastener in
place from the right side using the zipper foot.
Make little tabs from pieces of fabric 6cm × 8cm
(2¼in × 3¼in): iron under 1cm (½in) all around
and fold together to make 2cm × 5cm (¾in × 2in)
(seam allowances inside) and sew close to the
edge. Tack the tabs on to the right side over the
ends of the zip fastener and sew to the bag at the
short ends.

PENDANT

Cut out a flower motif from fabric A and sew on to
a piece of matching felt (or another strong fabric)
the same size using zigzag stitch, incorporating a
loop 8cm (3¼in) long from satin ribbon (placed
between the pieces before sewing together).
Thread glass beads on to the loop and knot the
pendant on to the zip fastener.

If you attach a cord or a ribbon to the tabs,
you can hang the bag up and use it as a
little handbag.

PATTERN PIECES	ZIP-FASTENED BAG		
1	Bag	1 × fabric A on the fold line (outer bag)	
		1 × fabric B on the fold line (inner bag/lining)	
	NOT ON THE PATTERN SHEET: MOBILE PHONE CASE		
1	Outer bag	21cm × 21cm (8¼in × 8¼in)	1 × fabric A
	Iron-on volume fleece in the centre, seam allowances remain free		
2	Inner lining	13cm × 21cm (5in × 8¼in)	1 × fabric B
	Volume fleece for outer bag	19cm × 19cm (7½in × 7½in)	

Mobile phone case

SEAM ALLOWANCES

1cm (½in) seam allowances included.

SEWING INSTRUCTIONS

Cut out all the pieces according to the instructions and reinforce with volume fleece or fleece interfacing as instructed.

Sew the hook-and-loop fastening to the right side of the fabric as shown in the diagram of the outer bag. Fold the outer bag up right sides together. Sew the side and base seams.

Turn right side out. Turn the raw edge with the hook-and-loop fastenings inside by 5cm (2in) along the edge of the fold line and tack in place. Fold the inner lining to 16cm × 10.5cm (6¼in × 4¼in), right side inside. Sew the side and base seams and turn out. Iron the seam allowance of the raw edge inwards.

Turn the outer bag inside out. Place the inner lining over it and sew around the turned-in trim of the outer bag by hand. Turn the mobile phone case right side out. Fold the ribbon for the karabiner hook into a loop and tack inside to the side seam. Topstitch around the top edge, following the width of the sewing machine foot, incorporating the ribbon for the karabiner hook at the same time. Thread the karabiner hook on to the loop.

You can individualise the mobile phone case with mother-of-pearl buttons or beads that you can sew on by hand, or make a decorative pendant by threading on little beads, crystals and a felt ball, for example.

LEVEL OF DIFFICULTY 2

SIZE
38cm × 54cm (15in × 21¼in)
(without handle)

MATERIALS
Fabric A (QTW1900-BLUE),
60cm (23½in)

Fabric B (QVM1800-RAIN),
60cm (23½in)

White sewing thread, e.g.
Coats Cotton number 50,
colour 2716

**PATTERN SHEET A
(LIGHT GREY)**

Large shoulder bag

When cutting out fabrics with large patterns, make sure that the motifs are evenly spaced. Arrange the fold so that a striking or large motif (here, the repeated design for fabric A) is centred and looks right when cut out, i.e. it is not cut into unnecessarily. The front and back pieces should be the same for the bag too. You may therefore need more fabric to achieve a nice, balanced look to the pattern.

For fabric A, mentioned above, the pattern fits exactly (placed twice next to each other across the width of the fabric) with the centre of the design. This is why, in this instance, the same amount of fabric is used as for fabric B with a small pattern.

SEAM AND HEM ALLOWANCES
For all seams and edges 1cm (½in).

SEWING INSTRUCTIONS

Cut out all pieces according to the pattern, marking the side lines and the centre of each pleat. Neaten around all the pieces using zigzag stitch.

For all four bag pieces, place the side lines of the pleats in the direction of the centre of the pleat, so that the side lines meet up to form a box pleat (see instructions on page 110). Iron the pleats and sew in place inside the seam allowance.

Lay the bag pieces from fabric A right sides together and tack. Sew the side and base seams in one go. Iron the seam allowances flat. Do the same thing with the bag pieces for fabric B. Pull bag piece B into bag piece A, right sides together. The side seams and the box pleats should match up. Sew outer bag A to inner bag B.

Leave open the holes for attaching the handles and 8cm (3¼in) for the opening for turning. Turn the bag right side out and iron. Close the opening for turning by hand.

Place a handle in fabric A against a handle in fabric B right sides together, tack and sew together along the long sides. Iron the seam allowances flat, turn out the handles and iron again.

Turn in the seam allowances for the holes for the handles and tack the handles into the openings. Sew a joining seam close to the edge.

PATTERN PIECES		
1	Bag	2 × fabric A on the fold line (for outer bag)
		2 × fabric B on the fold line (for inner bag)
2	Handle	2 × fabric A on the fold line (outer bag handle)
		2 × fabric B on the fold line (inner bag handle)

Camera case

SEAM ALLOWANCES

1cm (½in) seam allowances included.

SEWING INSTRUCTIONS

Cut out all the pieces according to the instructions and reinforce with volume fleece or fleece interfacing.

Tack the bag pieces together, right sides facing, and sew three of the sides together, leaving a 9cm (3½in) opening along the top short edge. Make sure the opening is exactly in the middle, as the bag flap will be inserted later at this point. Iron the seam allowances flat and cut off at an angle at the corners. Turn the bag out and iron.

Fold the drawstring channel to 5.5cm × 8cm (2¼in × 3¼in), right side inside. Sew together the short edges. Cut off the seam allowances at an angle at the corners. Turn right side out and iron. Topstitch the short sides from the right side, following the width of the sewing machine foot.

Tack the bag flaps together, right sides facing, sew together along both long sides and one short side.

Iron the seam allowances flat, cut off at an angle at the corners, turn out and iron again. Topstitch around the edge, following the width of the sewing machine foot, sewing up the raw edge at the same time.

Push the raw edge of the flap 2cm (¾in) down into the hole of the bag piece, so that the flap side in fabric A matches the bag side in fabric B. Fold together the drawstring channel and pin to the centre of the opening of the bag piece. Tack the flap and the drawstring channel in place. At this point, you need to decide which side will be the bag outer side: put the drawstring channel on the side that is to be the outer side (here, for example, the checked side).

Sew the flap and the drawstring channel to the bag piece, both close to the edge and following the width of the sewing machine foot. This will close up the seam for turning at the same time.

Fold together the bag piece (outer side lies against the inside).

Insert a velvet ribbon for the fastening, so that it is sewn in at the same time, 7cm (2¾in) from the top edge, with the velvet side towards the fold. Close both side seams with a small lockstitch, following the width of the sewing machine foot. Fold under the excess ends of the velvet ribbon and sew to the edges of the bag using a narrow zigzag stitch. Sew the darts for the base: place the corners at the base of the bag in such a way that the side seam runs along the centre of the base in the direction of the tips of the corners. Sew the darts at right angles to the side seam 1.5cm (⅝in) from the tip of the corner (see instructions on page 109).

Turn the bag right side out.

Thread through the cord and knot.

Instead of the velvet ribbon, you could attach a hook-and-loop fastening. A button fastening would also be suitable: find a matching button and sew it on to the bag piece. Instead of a buttonhole, use a loop of narrow elastic, which is sewn into the seam when sewing together the flap.

		NOT ON THE PATTERN SHEET:		
	1a	Outer bag	14cm × 34cm (5½in × 13½in)	1 × fabric A, iron-on volume fleece
	1b	Inner bag	14cm × 34cm (5½in × 13½in)	1 × fabric B
	2a	Bag flap	11cm × 18cm (4¼in × 7in)	1 × fabric A, reinforced with fleece interfacing
	2b	Bag flap	11cm × 18cm (4¼in × 7in)	1 × fabric B
PATTERN PIECES	3	Drawstring channel	11cm × 8cm (4¼in × 3⅛in)	1 × fabric B, reinforced with fleece interfacing
	4	Volume fleece	12cm × 32cm (4¾in × 12½in) for bag piece A	
	5	Fleece interfacing	9cm × 16cm (3½in × 6¼in) for flap piece A	
			9cm × 6cm (3½in × 2¼in) for drawstring channel	

LEVEL OF DIFFICULTY 2

SIZE
12cm × 15cm (4¾in × 6in)

MATERIALS
Fabric A (QTW1800-RED),
14cm (5½in)

Fabric B (QTW2200-BLUSH),
14cm (5½in)

Volume fleece, single-sided
iron-on, 12cm (4¾in)

Fleece interfacing, 9cm (3½in)

Velvet ribbon, matching
colour, 1.5cm (⅝in) wide,
14cm (5½in)

Cord, matching colour,
70cm (27½in)

White sewing thread, e.g.
Coats Cotton number 50,
colour 2716

STYLISH LIVING

Comfortable floor cushion

LEVEL OF DIFFICULTY 2

SIZE
Diameter 50cm (19¾in), height 20cm (7¾in)

MATERIALS
Fabric A (QAH2400-ZINNI), 55cm × 55cm
(21¾in × 21¾in)

Fabric B (QAH2600-CHOCO), 55cm × 55cm
(21¾in × 21¾in)

Or just one of these fabrics if you prefer, 55cm
(21¾in) (top and bottom the same)

Fabric C (QVM1600-GRAPE), 50cm (19¾in)

Iron-on fleece interfacing for reinforcing all
of the pattern pieces

Zip fastener, 60cm (23½in), e.g. Opti S40,
natural, colour 0089

Red sewing thread, e.g. Coats Cotton
number 50, colour 7810

For the filling:

Styropor granules (Rayher, 3–5mm [¼in]),
0.9–1kg (2lb), equivalent to approximately
45–50 litres

Light cotton fabric for the inner cushion

SEAM AND HEM ALLOWANCES
For all seams and edges 1cm (½in) (already included).

SEWING INSTRUCTIONS
Cut out all pieces according to the instructions,
reinforce with fleece interfacing and neaten
around the edges using zigzag stitch.

Place both side pieces 2 together, right sides
facing. Tack along one long side and sew together,
securing the seam after 10.5cm (4¼in) with three
to four backstitches (sew a bar tack). Set to a
larger stitch width (e.g. 4mm [¼in]) and sew
again. After 60cm (23½in) (10.5cm [4¼in] before
the raw edge), adjust the stitch width back again
and make a second bar tack. Sew the seam using
normal stitch length. Iron the seam allowance flat
on the reverse.
Place the zip fastener on the ironed seam with
the reverse side uppermost and tack in place by
hand. Undo the seam between the two bar tacks.
Sew in the zip fastener from the right side using
the zipper foot 7mm (⅜in) from the seam edge.
Remove the tacking threads.

Sew together the side pieces (1 + 2) to form a
ring: lay the short edges on top of one another,
right sides together, tack both seams and sew.
Iron the seam allowances flat.

Tack the side piece to the top piece, right sides
together, and sew in place.
The sewing will be most accurate when the top
piece is lying flat against the sewing machine
table, wrong side down, and the side piece is on
top, right sides together. This is the best way to
ensure that the pieces stay flat when sewn
together. Iron the seam allowances flat. Open the
zip fastener a little and sew the other side to the
bottom piece in the same way. Turn the cushion
right side out.

For instructions on filling the inner cushion with
styropor granules, see page 111.

PATTERN PIECES				
NOT ON THE PATTERN SHEET:				
1	Top and bottom piece	Circle, 52cm (20½in) diameter	1 × fabric A	
		Reinforce with fleece interfacing	1 × fabric B	
2	Side piece 1	22cm × 80.5cm (8¾in × 31¾in)	1 × fabric C	
		Reinforce with fleece interfacing		
3	Side piece 2	12cm × 80.5cm (4¾in × 31¾in)	2 × fabric C	
		Reinforce with fleece interfacing		
4	Fleece interfacing	Reinforce all pieces including seam allowances		

Large bolster

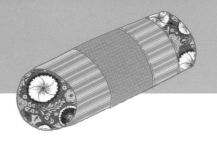

LEVEL OF DIFFICULTY 2

SIZE
Length 80cm (31½in), diameter 25cm (9¾in)

MATERIALS
Fabric A (QTW1800-RED), 85cm (33½in)

Fabric B (QAH2400-ZINNI), 30cm (11¾in)

Iron-on fleece interfacing for reinforcing all of the pattern pieces

Double-sided adhesive web, e.g. Vliesofix for the flower appliqués

Zip fastener, 60cm (23½in), e.g. Opti S40, dark red, colour 0752

Natural-coloured sewing thread, e.g. Coats Cotton number 50, colour 1418

Natural-coloured embroidery yarn, e.g. Coats Creative, colour 1418

For the filling:

Styropor granules (Rayher, 3–5mm [¼in]), 0.7–0.8kg(1¾lb), equivalent to approximately 35 litres

Light cotton fabric for the inner cushion

SEAM AND HEM ALLOWANCES
For all seams and edges 1cm (½in) (already included).

SEWING INSTRUCTIONS

Cut out all pieces according to the instructions, reinforce with fleece interfacing and neaten around the edges using zigzag stitch.
From the remnant of fabric A, select five flowers. Cut out roughly and iron on adhesive web. Cut around the flower motifs and arrange as desired on the centre piece. The distance to the bottom edge (82cm [32¼in] long) of the fabric should be 28cm (11in) and the distance between the flowers should be approximately 5cm (2in).

SEWING AROUND THE FLOWERS AND EMBROIDERING THE STEMS

Mark the stems on the fabric from the bottom edge in the direction of the grain up to the flowers. Select a stronger sewing needle (90–100) and use the natural-coloured embroidery yarn as a top thread. Check the size of the stitch on a remnant of fabric, stitch length approximately 3.5mm (¼in). If necessary, relax the top thread tension a little.

Sew the stem once, then sew twice around the shape of the flowers. Change the sewing needle and thread again.
Tack the top and bottom edges (82cm [32¼in]) of the centre piece together, right sides facing, and sew together, securing the seam after 11cm (4¼in) with three to four backstitches (sew bar tack). Set to a larger stitch width (e.g. 4mm [¼in]) and sew again. After 60cm (23½in) (11cm [4¼in] before the raw edge), adjust the stitch width back again and make a second bar tack. Sew the seam using normal stitch length. Iron the seam allowance flat on the reverse.
Place the zip fastener on the ironed seam with the reverse side uppermost and tack in place by hand. Undo the seam between the two bar tacks. Sew in the zip fastener from the right side using the zipper foot 7mm (⅜in) from the seam edge. Remove the tacking threads and open the zip fastener.

Turn the centre piece inside out and tack to the side pieces, right sides together, and sew in place. The sewing will be most accurate when the top piece is lying flat against the sewing machine table, wrong side down, and the side piece is on top. This is the best way to ensure that the pieces stay flat when sewn together.
Iron the seam allowances flat. Turn the cushion right side out.

For instructions on filling the inner cushion with styropor granules, see page 111.

PATTERN PIECES		NOT ON THE PATTERN SHEET:		
	1	Centre piece	80.5cm × 82cm (31¾in × 32¼in)	1 × fabric A
			Reinforce with fleece interfacing	
	2	Side piece	Circle, 27cm (10¾in) diameter	2 × fabric B
			Reinforce with fleece interfacing	
	3	Fleece interfacing	Reinforce all pieces including seam allowances	

Cosy cushions

LEVEL OF DIFFICULTY 1

SIZE

50cm × 50cm (19¾in × 19¾in) and
35cm × 70cm (13¾in × 27½in)

MATERIALS

Two pieces of fabric 52cm × 52cm
(20½in × 20½in)

Matching sewing thread, e.g. Coats Cotton
number 50

Zip fastener, 40cm (15¾in), e.g. Opti S40,
matching colour

CUSHION 1

QAH2400-ZINNI, QTW1800-PINK (reverse)

CUSHION 2

QVM1800-MILK, thirty small fabric remnants,
5cm × 3cm (2in × 1¼in)

CUSHION 3

QQVM1700-GRAPE, nine circles of
10cm (4in) diameter

Double-sided iron-on fleece interfacing

Natural-coloured embroidery yarn, e.g. Coats
Creative number 16, colour 1418

CUSHION 4

Fabric A (QTW1900-BLUE)

Fabric B (QTW2200-BLUE)

Fabric C (QTW1800-RED)

Fabric D (QTW1800-BLUE) (reverse)

Cushion covers are very easy to sew and provide a lot of scope for creativity. They can easily be changed, giving any room a quick makeover.

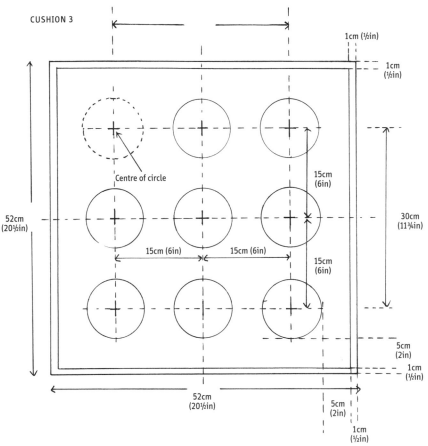

CUSHION 3

1cm (½in)

1cm (½in)

Centre of circle

52cm (20½in)

15cm (6in)

15cm (6in)

15cm (6in)

15cm (6in)

15cm (6in)

30cm (11¾in)

5cm (2in)

1cm (½in)

52cm (20½in)

5cm (2in)

1cm (½in)

CUSHION 4

Includes 1cm (½in) seam allowance

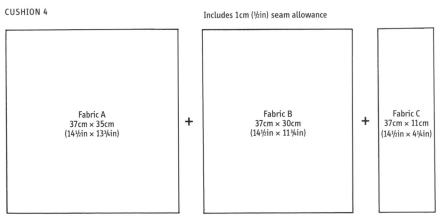

Fabric A
37cm × 35cm
(14½in × 13¾in)

+

Fabric B
37cm × 30cm
(14½in × 11¾in)

+

Fabric C
37cm × 11cm
(14½in × 4¼in)

SEWING INSTRUCTIONS
STEP 1

Always attach the appliqués (as for cushion 3) before sewing the two cushion pieces together. Work out the position of the motifs and mark up on the front half of the cushion.

Iron on the motifs using double-sided adhesive fleece interfacing. Either sew on the motifs in the traditional way using a narrow zigzag stitch around the edge or use thicker embroidery yarn to do freehand embroidery stitches. For more detailed instructions, see the strawberry appliqués on the girls' dress on page 30 or the strawberry bag on page 40.

Embroidered motifs secured with just a centre seam (as for cushion 2) should not be too large, otherwise they will become floppy. The slight fraying of the raw edges is intentional and can look 'shabby chic', if the cushion is not designed for too much use. Simply pull off any long threads at the start.

If the cushion is intended for everyday use and frequent washing, a lightweight, matching fleece interfacing should be ironed on before cutting out the little rectangles. Make sure that this bonds really well with the fabric to prevent too much fraying.

For cushions made from various fabrics placed together (as for cushion 4), cut out the pieces of fabric with a 1cm (½in) seam allowance, neaten using zigzag stitch and sew together, right sides facing. Iron the seam allowances flat and topstitch on the right side depending on the desired look. Sew on decorative ribbons (width or height of the cushion + seam allowance) before sewing the two cushion halves together, so that the ends of the ribbons can be sewn neatly into the seams later.

STEP 2

Once the cushion pieces are decorated or placed together, neaten all the raw edges using zigzag stitch. Then place the two pieces of fabric right sides together and tack together along one side (bottom edge, zip fastening edge), securing the seam after 6cm (2¼in) with three to four backstitches (sew bar tack). Set to a larger stitch width (e.g. 4mm [¼in]) and sew again. After 40cm (15¾in) (6cm [2¼in] before the raw edge), adjust the stitch width back again and make a second bar tack. Sew the seam using normal stitch length. Iron the seam allowance flat on the reverse.
Place the zip fastener on the ironed seam with the reverse side uppermost and tack in place by hand. Undo the seam between the two bar tacks. Sew in the zip fastener from the right side using the zipper foot 7mm (⅜in) from the seam edge.

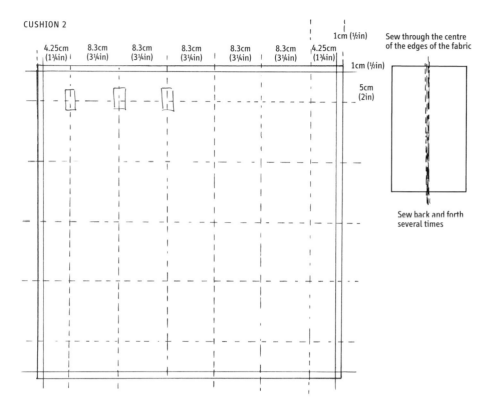

CUSHION 2

4.25cm (1¾in) | 8.3cm (3¼in) | 8.3cm (3¼in) | 8.3cm (3¼in) | 8.3cm (3¼in) | 8.3cm (3¼in) | 4.25cm (1¾in)

1cm (½in)

1cm (½in)

5cm (2in)

Sew through the centre of the edges of the fabric

Sew back and forth several times

Remove the tacking threads, leaving the zip fastener open by approximately 10cm (4in), and sew around the remaining sides. Iron the seam allowances flat and turn the cushion right side out.

Decorative table runner

LEVEL OF DIFFICULTY 1

SIZE
45cm × 1.5m (17¾in × 59in)

MATERIALS
Fabric A (QTW1900-BLUE), 1.55m (61in)
(enough for two pieces)

White sewing thread, e.g. Coats Cotton
number 50, colour 2716

CUTTING OUT
With large patterns watch out for symmetrical or
centred motifs.

SEAM ALLOWANCES
For all raw edges 3cm (1¼in).

SEWING INSTRUCTIONS
Cut out the table runner according to the
instructions. Turn up the long edges twice (1.5cm
[⅝in] each), iron and tack. Topstitch close to the
edge. Turn up the short edges twice, iron and
tack. Take care to ensure that the edges do not jut
out at the sides. Sew in place close to the edge in
the same way.

Sew a reversible table runner – simply cut out
two different fabrics with 1.5cm (⅝in) seam
allowance, sew together, right sides facing,
leaving a 10cm (4in) opening for turning. Iron
the seam allowances flat, turn right side out
and close up the opening by hand. Iron the
folded edges neatly and tack. Sew 1.5cm (⅝in)
from the edge all around.
If you sew two identical reversible runners
(1.55m [61in] fabric needed per runner), there
will be less waste and lots of possibilities for
decorating your table.

Practical shopping bag

LEVEL OF DIFFICULTY 2

SIZE
45cm × 40cm × 12cm (17¾in × 15¾in × 4¾in)
(height × width × depth)

MATERIALS
Fabric A (QAH2600-CHOCO), 75cm (29½in)

Fabric B (QVM1600-GRAPE), 85cm (33½in)

Pink sewing thread, e.g. Coats Cotton
number 50, colour 2511

**PATTERN SHEET B
(BLACK)**

Place the pattern pieces for the bag (side piece – bag – side piece) directly next to one another without a seam allowance (the far left and far right edges must of course be given a 1cm [½in] seam allowance) and cut out the bag over the whole width of the fabric. Mark all the edges of the pieces well with chalk or an ironed-in crease.

Using this method means that you have to close up only one seam, resulting in hardly any waste, plus you achieve a nice effect with the fabric pattern encasing the bag without any breaks. The amount of fabric stated above has been worked out with this method in mind.

SEAM AND HEM ALLOWANCES
For all seams and edges 1cm (½in).

SEWING INSTRUCTIONS
Cut out all the pieces according to the pattern and the instructions.
Neaten around all the pieces using zigzag stitch. Tack the side seam of the outer bag right sides together and sew. Iron the seam allowances flat. Iron all four edges from the right side and topstitch close to the edge.

Tack the base of the outer bag to the body of the bag, right sides together. First sew in place the long edges, then the short edges. Iron the seam allowances flat and topstitch around the base close to the edge on the right side.
Repeat the same process for the parts in fabric B for the inner bag.

Pull bag piece B into bag piece A, right sides together. The side seams should match up. Sew outer bag A to inner bag B, leaving a 10cm (4in) opening for turning. Turn the bag right side out and iron. Tack the opening for turning.

Turn under the top edge of the bag at the marked fold line by 3.5cm (1½in) and sew in place close to the edge to form a channel for the handle and closing up the opening for turning.

Handle: iron the seam allowances for the long sides to the reverse. Fold the handle in half along the length, iron and tack, turning the seam allowances inwards. Topstitch close to the edge on the right side to form a band 3cm (1¼in) wide. Pull the band for the handle through the channel and sew together with a 1cm (½in) overlap. Pull the band for the handle round, so that the seam is hidden, then sew in place on the right side into the seam allowance for the side seam.

This bag has no interfacing or reinforcing, which means that it can be folded up very small and can carry a lot of shopping if required.
If you would prefer a bag that will stand up on its own, reinforce all the pattern pieces with firm fleece interfacing and insert a base made from strong card or plastic.

PATTERN PIECES	1	Bag	2 × fabric A (for outer bag)
			2 × fabric B (for inner bag)
	2	Side piece	2 × fabric A (for outer bag)
			2 × fabric B (for inner bag)
	3	Base	1 × fabric A (for outer bag)
			1 × fabric B (for inner bag)
		NOT ON THE PATTERN SHEET:	
	4	Handle	1 × fabric B (cut 8cm × 1.07m [3¼in × 42¼in], allowance of 1cm [½in] included)

Placemat and serviette

LEVEL OF DIFFICULTY 1

SIZE
Placemat 35cm (13¾in) diameter
Mushroom serviette 45cm × 45cm
(17¾in × 17¾in)

MATERIALS

PLACEMAT
Fabric A (QTW1800-BLUE), 38cm (15in)

Fabric B (QVM1700-GRAPE), 38cm (15in)

Fleece interfacing, 38cm × 38cm (15in × 15in)

Double-sided adhesive web, e.g. Vliesofix
for appliqué

White sewing thread, e.g. Coats Cotton
number 50, colour 2716

Natural-coloured embroidery yarn, e.g. Coats
Creative, colour 1418

MUSHROOM SERVIETTE
Fabric A (QTW1800-BLUE), 48cm × 48cm
(19in × 19in) (1.5cm [⅝in] seam
allowance included)

Fabric B (QVM1700-GRAPE), small remnant
for mushroom top appliqué

Fabric C (QVM1800-MILK), small remnant for
mushroom stalk appliqué

Double-sided adhesive web, e.g. Vliesofix
for appliqué

Lace trim, 1.82m (71¾in)

White sewing thread, e.g. Coats Cotton
number 50, colour 2716

Natural-coloured embroidery yarn, e.g. Coats
Creative, colour 1418

PATTERN SHEET A (TURQUOISE)

Placemat with heart motif

CUTTING OUT
Cut out all the pieces according to the instructions.
1cm (½in) seam allowance included. Reinforce
both sides of fabric with fleece interfacing,
avoiding the seam allowances.

SEWING INSTRUCTIONS
Transfer the heart motif froma the pattern sheet
to fabric B and iron on to the centre of fabric
circle A using adhesive web.
Place the circles right sides together, tack and
sew, leaving an opening for turning of 8cm
(3¼in). Iron the seam allowances flat. Turn the
placemat right side out. Iron the fold line edges
neatly on top of one another and tack the opening
for turning. Sew round close to the edge and then
1cm (½in) from the edge, closing up the opening
for turning as you go.

Sew around the shape of the heart by machine:
insert a stronger sewing needle (90–100) and use
the embroidery yarn for the top and bottom
threads. Check the size of the stitch on a remnant
of fabric, stitch length approximately 3.5mm
(¼in). If necessary, relax the top thread tension a
little. Sew roughly over the shape of the heart a
few times. Change the sewing needle and
thread again.

NOT ON THE PATTERN SHEET:

1	Top side	1 × fabric A (cut circle, 38cm [15in] diameter)
2	Reverse side	1 × fabric B (cut circle, 38cm [15in] diameter)

Mushroom serviette

CUTTING OUT
Cut out the serviette as instructed. Turn up the
seam allowances around the edge twice, iron and
tack. Tack the lace trim under the edge, leaving
approximately 1cm (½in) overlapping.

SEWING INSTRUCTIONS
Sew the edge from the right side (single or double),
catching the lace into the sewing.

Transfer the mushroom motif from the pattern
sheet to fabrics B and C. First iron the stalk and
then the top of the mushroom on to one corner of
the serviette using adhesive web.

Sew around the shape of the mushroom by
machine: insert a stronger sewing needle
(90–100) and use the embroidery yarn for the top
thread. Check the size of the stitch on a remnant
of fabric, stitch length approximately 3.5mm (¼in). If
necessary, relax the top thread tension a little.
Sew roughly over the shape of the mushroom
once or twice with the embroidery yarn.

Embroidered flower serviette

LEVEL OF DIFFICULTY 1

SIZE
45cm × 45cm (17¾in × 17¾in)

MATERIALS
Fabric A (QTW1800-PINK), 49cm × 49cm (19¼in × 19¼in) (2cm [¾in] seam allowance included)

White sewing thread, e.g. Coats Cotton number 50, colour 2716

Natural-coloured and red embroidery yarns, e.g. Coats Creative, colours 1418 and 7810

PATTERN SHEET A (BROWN)

CUTTING OUT
Cut out the serviette as instructed on page 67.

SEWING INSTRUCTIONS
Turn up two opposite edges twice by 1cm (½in) each, iron and tack. Topstitch close to the edge. Turn up the other two edges twice, iron and tack. Make sure that the edges do not jut out at the sides. Sew in place close to the edge.

SEWING ON THE EMBROIDERY MOTIF
Transfer the shape for the red embroidery yarn from the pattern sheet to one corner of the serviette – position the centre of the flower 7cm (2¾in) away from both edges. Insert a stronger sewing needle (90–100) and use the red embroidery yarn for the top thread. Check the size of the stitch on a remnant of fabric, stitch length approximately 3.5mm (¼in). If necessary, relax the top thread tension a little. Sew roughly over the shape of the flower twice with the red embroidery yarn. Transfer the shape for the natural-coloured embroidery yarn on to the serviette.
Change to the natural-coloured embroidery yarn and sew over again, slightly offset, one to two times.

Placemat, bread basket and coaster

LEVEL OF DIFFICULTY 1

SIZE
Bread basket 16cm × 18cm (6¼in × 7in),
height 6cm (2¼in)
Placemat 35cm × 45cm (13¾in × 17¾in)
Coaster 12cm (4¾in) diameter

MATERIALS

BREAD BASKET
Fabric A (QVM1300-MILK), 40cm × 42cm
(15¾in × 16½in)

Felting, 5–7mm (¼in) thick, 28cm × 30cm
(11in × 11¾in)

Natural-coloured sewing thread, e.g. Coats
Cotton number 50, colour 1418

PLACEMAT AND COASTER
Fabric A (QVM1800-GERAN), 19cm × 19cm
(7½in × 7½in), reinforced with fleece interfacing

Fleece interfacing, 19cm × 19cm (7½in × 7½in)

Felting, 5–7mm (¼in) thick, 35cm × 45cm
(13¾in × 17¾in) and circle with 12cm (4¾in)
diameter

Natural-coloured sewing thread, e.g. Coats
Cotton number 50, colour 1418

PATTERN SHEET
B (LILAC) + A (TURQUOISE)

Bread basket

CUTTING OUT
Cut out the pieces according to the instructions.

SEWING INSTRUCTIONS
Fold the sides of the felt basket upwards at the
fold line (right sides of the felt inside), with the
side seams matching. Sew the side seams
together using a narrow zigzag stitch from the top
edge towards the base. Turn the basket out.

Fold the sides of the inner felt basket upwards at
the fold line (right sides of the felt inside), with
the side seams matching. Tack the side seams and
sew together from the top edge towards the base.
Neaten the edges together using zigzag stitch.
Iron under the top edge by 2cm (¾in) to the
wrong side, turn up 1cm (½in) and topstitch close
to the edge.
Put the inner basket into the felt basket and turn
back the top edge by 3cm (1¼in) over the edge
of the felt.

Placemat and coaster

CUTTING OUT
Cut out the felt pieces as instructed.

SEWING INSTRUCTIONS
Transfer the heart motif from the pattern sheet to
the centre of fabric A and cut out. Transfer the
small heart motif from the pattern sheet to the
large heart cut-out piece and cut out.
Tack the motifs centred on the felt placemat and
coaster and embroider the edges using a narrow
zigzag stitch.

Instead of tacking the motifs, they can also be
easily stuck on using a fabric adhesive stick
(e.g. Prym). The adhesive can be washed out
and becomes transparent when dry.

PATTERN PIECES		
1	Felt basket	1 × felt (without seam allowances)
2	Inner basket	1 × fabric, same cut, but at the top edges cut
		5cm (2in) (3cm [1¼in] turn up + 2cm [¾in] seam allowance),
		cut with 1cm (½in) seam allowance at the side edges

Fashionable apron

SEAM AND HEM ALLOWANCES

Side seams for apron piece 2cm (¾in).
For all other seams and edges 1cm (½in).

SEWING INSTRUCTIONS

Cut out all pieces according to the instructions. Mark the side lines of the pleats.

Fold the apron piece (right side of the fabric inside), so that the pleat lines match up. Iron the pleat lines as shown on the pattern to 10cm (4in) long. Tack along the pleats for approximately 5cm (2in), iron the depth of the pleat flat and secure inside the seam allowances by topstitching.

Iron under the side seams of the apron piece 2cm (¾in) to the wrong side. Turn up 1cm (½in) and tack. Sew close to the edge.

Place the hem border pieces right sides together and tack. Sew the sides and the bottom edge. Cut the seam allowances at an angle at the corners and iron flat. Turn the border right side out, turn up the top seam allowances 1cm (½in) towards the inside and iron.

Tack the bottom edge of the apron (hem border) to the raw top edge of the border with the turned-up seam allowances; the side seams should match up. Sew the hem border from the right side close to the edge. Make sure that the edge of the hem border on the reverse side is also incorporated.

Place the waistband pieces right sides together, tack the top edge and sew. Iron the seam allowances flat, iron under the side seam allowances to the wrong side and tack. Tack the front bottom edge of the waistband to the apron piece, right sides together, with the seam allowances remaining folded in. Topstitch the waistband to the apron piece. Fold the waistband up and iron the seam allowances into the waistband. Turn in the seam allowances on the reverse of the waistband.

Tack the reverse of the waistband in place, so that it can be topstitched on the right side close to the edge in the seam.

Fold the ties in half along the length, wrong sides together, and sew together, leaving one short side open for turning. Iron the seam allowances flat and turn the tie right side out. Push out the corners using a blunt needle or a pen. Iron again from the right side to form a neat edge at the fold line.

Pin and tack the ties in place with the raw edges inserted 2.5cm (1in) into the open waistband pieces. Topstitch both ties from the right side into the waistband close to the edge, closing up the open sides of the waistband at the same time. Sew a rectangle on to the tie join at the back of the apron to secure each tie well.

PATTERN PIECES			
	1	Apron piece	1 × fabric A on the fold line
	2	Hem border	2 × fabric B on the fold line
	3	Waistband	2 × fabric B on the fold line
	NOT ON THE PATTERN SHEET:		
	4	Ties	2 × fabric B (cut 10.5cm × 1.12m [4¼in × 44in], seam allowance of 1cm [½in] included)

LEVEL OF DIFFICULTY 2

SIZE
Standard size

MATERIALS
Fabric A (QVM1600-GRAPE),
80cm (31½in)

Fabric B (QVM1500-GRAPE),
40cm (15¾in)

Pink sewing thread, e.g.
Coats Cotton number 50,
colour 2511

**PATTERN SHEET B
(PINK)**

SWEET DREAMS

Fabulous patchwork quilt

LEVEL OF DIFFICULTY 3

SIZE
2m × 1.5m (78¾in × 59in)

MATERIALS
Fabric A (QTW1800-RED), 1.02m × 1.72m (40¼in × 67¾in) (use the cross-grain)

Fabric B (QTW2100-AQUA), 1.02m × 1.72m (40¼in × 67¾in) (use the cross-grain), 32cm × 32cm (12½in × 12½in), 2 ×, total fabric used 2.1m (82¾in)

Fabric C (QVM1600-RAIN), 62cm × 1.32m (24½in × 52in) (use the cross-grain), 12cm × 1.32m (4¾in × 52in), 2 ×, total fabric used 1.4m (55in) (cut from top remnant. If the stripes are to run vertically as in the photo, they must be placed together with three to four 12cm-high (4¾in) strips, so that the pattern continues along the seam crossovers)

Fabric D (QVM1800-GERAN), 32cm × 52cm, (12½in × 20½in) 2 ×, total fabric used 70cm (27½in)

Fabric E (QTW1800-PINK), 32cm × 72cm, (12½in × 28¼in) 2 ×, total fabric used 70cm (27½in)

Fabric F (QVM1800-RAIN), 32cm × 22cm, (12½in × 8¾in) 2 ×, total fabric used 35cm (13¾in)

Fabric G (QVM1300-MILK), 32cm × 12cm, (12½in × 4¾in) 4 ×, total fabric used 24cm (9½in)

Volume fleece, 2m × 1.5m (78¾in × 59in)

White sewing thread, e.g. Coats Cotton number 50, colour 2716

DIAGRAM PAGE 78

SEAM ALLOWANCE

All measurements include a 1cm (½in) seam allowance.

SEWING INSTRUCTIONS

Cut out all pieces according to the instructions. Make up the reverse: place the two large pieces of fabric A and fabric B on top of one another, tack along one 1.72m (67¾in) long side and sew together. Iron the seam allowances flat. Iron the long (2.02m [79½in]) sides 11cm (4¼in) under to the wrong side, making it easier later to turn over to the top side.

TOP SIDE

To maintain the overall look, it is best to start by laying together, in little piles, the pieces in each row across the quilt. The lengthways running 10cm-wide (4in) side strips for the top side can be ignored, as they are a part of the reverse side. First sew together the pieces going across the quilt. Tack right sides together as in the detailed diagram on page 78 and sew together the lengthways seams one after another. Iron the seam allowances flat.

The completed cross strips for the top side are 1.3m (51¼in) wide (1.32m [52in] with seam allowances). Next, place one cross strip after another as in the diagram, right sides together, tack and sew together. Iron the seam allowances flat.

Place the long sides of the top side and the reverse side together, right sides facing, tack and sew together along both sides. Leave the quilt turned the wrong side out and with the help of the creases on the reverse side, pull the pieces flat on top of one another. The 10cm-wide (4in) side strips are now lying on the top side, with the top and reverse sides lying flat on top of one another. Lay the volume fleece exactly on top and secure with pins or tacking thread. Tack the short sides together incorporating the volume fleece. Completely sew one short side (the volume fleece is sewn in place at the same time), leaving an opening for turning of approximately 30cm (11¾in) on the other side.

Remove the pins and tacking thread and turn the quilt right side out. Iron the edges of the fold line. Secure the volume fleece in place again from the right side along the long sides. Close up the opening for turning by hand.

Sew the quilt from the right side into the seam 10cm (4in) from the edge, incorporating the fleece in the sewing. Remove the tacking thread.

If you wish, you can now choose to sew further seams, or place appliqués in the large areas with small patterns.

Alternatively, you could embroider on motifs by hand or by machine (e.g. the flower motif for the women's pyjamas on page 90) in the red corners of the quilt. These can then be seen from the reverse side too and look very decorative.

Another variation is to further subdivide the areas in the diagram crossways and lengthways or join them together.

Diagram for patchwork quilt

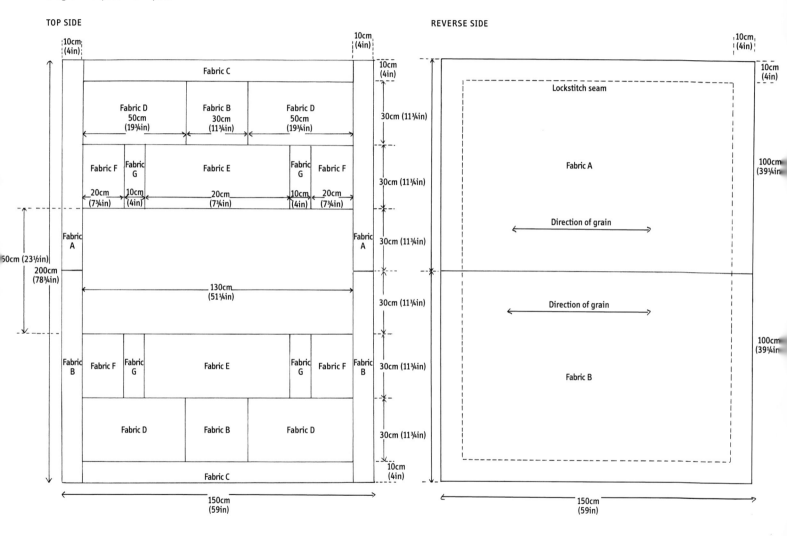

TOP SIDE

10cm
(4in)

10cm
(4in)

Fabric C

Fabric D
50cm
(19¾in)

Fabric B
30cm
(11¾in)

Fabric D
50cm
(19¾in)

10cm
(4in)

30cm (11¾in)

Fabric F

Fabric
G

Fabric E

Fabric
G

Fabric F

30cm (11¾in)

20cm
(7¾in)

10cm
(4in)

20cm
(7¾in)

10cm
(4in)

20cm
(7¾in)

Fabric
A

Fabric
A

30cm (11¾in)

60cm (23½in)

130cm
(51¼in)

200cm
(78¾in)

30cm (11¾in)

Fabric
B

Fabric F

Fabric
G

Fabric E

Fabric
G

Fabric F

Fabric
B

30cm (11¾in)

Fabric D

Fabric B

Fabric D

30cm (11¾in)

Fabric C

10cm
(4in)

150cm
(59in)

REVERSE SIDE

10cm
(4in)

10cm
(4in)

Lockstitch seam

10cm
(4in)

Fabric A

100cm
(39¼in)

Direction of grain

Direction of grain

Fabric B

100cm
(39¼in)

150cm
(59in)

Patterned tidy
Details on page 80

Patterned tidy

LEVEL OF DIFFICULTY 3

SIZE

55cm × 42cm (21¾in × 16½in)

MATERIALS

Fabric A (QTW1700-RED), 1m (39¼in)

Fabric B (QTW2200-BLUSH), 50cm (19¾in)

Fabric C (QTW1800-RED), 25cm (9¾in)

Volume fleece, single-sided iron-on, 45cm (17¾in)

Fleece interfacing, 40cm (15¾in)

Velvet ribbon, 1.5cm (½in) wide, matching colour, 70cm (27½in)

White sewing thread, e.g. Coats Cotton number 50, colour 2716

Elastic, 5mm (¼in) wide

Large button, matching colour

SEAM ALLOWANCES

1cm (½in) seam allowances included.

SEWING INSTRUCTIONS

Cut out all the pieces according to the instructions and reinforce as instructed with volume fleece or fleece interfacing.

N.B. When cutting the pieces from fabric A, make sure that the centre of each piece sits on the same lengthways stripe. Then the stripes on the pieces will match up exactly when sewn together later. Tack together the outer and inner sides of the tidy, right sides together, and sew together so that the top short side is closed up 2.5cm (1in) away from the edge all along. Iron the seam allowances flat and turn the tidy right side out. Iron the top seam allowances inside.

Tack together the pocket pieces for the large pocket, right sides together. Sew together the pocket on three sides, leaving one long side open. Iron the seam allowances flat. Turn out and iron. Neaten together the bottom raw edge using zigzag stitch.

Fold the trim of the small pocket inside by 2.5cm (1in), turn up the seam allowance by 1cm (½in) and topstitch close to the edge from the right side. Turn up the remaining seam allowances and iron. Tack the small pocket to the large pocket, 1.2cm (½in) from the bottom, raw edge of the large pocket and 2cm (¾in) away from each side. Stitch the small pocket in place close to the edge. Work out the size of the pocket compartments for the small pocket and sew dividing seams.

Ironed pleats for the large pocket: fold the seam allowance to the wrong side at the bottom edge of the large pocket and iron. Iron the right and left pocket sides 2cm (¾in) to the inside and 1cm (½in) to the outside. Secure the ironed pleats with pins.

Fold up the bottom edge of the tidy (fabric B is on the inside), having measured 33cm (13in) from the fold line, and pin in place.

Place the pocket element with the folded-in and pinned and ironed pleats in the centre of the folded-down part of the tidy.

		NOT ON THE PATTERN SHEET:		
	1a	Tidy outer side	92cm × 47cm (36¼in × 18½in)	1 × fabric A, iron-on volume fleece
	1b	Tidy inner side	92cm × 47cm (36¼in × 18½in)	1 × fabric B
	2	Pocket, large	25cm × 42cm (9¾in × 16½in)	2 × fabric C, reinforce one piece with fleece interfacing
	3	Pocket, small	18cm × 38cm (7in × 15in)	1 × fabric A, reinforce with fleece interfacing
	4	Volume fleece for outer side	90cm × 45cm (35½in × 17¾in)	1 × fabric A
	5	Fleece interfacing for large pocket	23cm × 40cm (9in × 15¾in)	
		Fleece interfacing for small pocket	16cm × 36cm (6¼in × 14¼in)	

Left margin label: PATTERN PIECES

Tack the side seams in place and sew close to the edge, so that in the second step, the bottom edge of the pocket element can also be sewn in place close to the edge, flat and with the ironed pleats on top of one another.

Fold the tidy down again at the fold line, this time with fabric A inside. Tack the edges lying on top of one another and sew together. Turn the tidy right side out.

Fold three equal-sized pieces of velvet ribbon into loops approximately 5cm (2in) long. Pin into the open, top edge of the tidy. Tack the edge and sew together close to the edge.
Turn up the excess seam allowances at the top part of the tidy towards the centre and sew in place close to the edge.
Sew little loops of velvet ribbon to the middle of the pocket using fine zigzag stitch. Sew on a loop of elastic and a suitable button to close the tidy.

You can also hang the tidy between the mattress and the bed, which avoids the need for a loop for hanging.
If you want to, you can also attach a hook-and-loop fastening to the reverse of the top edge, so that the tidy can be secured around a metal frame, as shown here.

Bed linen for girls

LEVEL OF DIFFICULTY 2

SIZE
Quilt cover 1.3m × 95cm (51¼in × 37½in)
Pillows 40cm × 60cm (15¾in × 23½in) with
reversible, slip-on pillowcases

MATERIALS
Fabric A (QTW1800-PINK), 2m (78¾in)

Fabric B (QVM1800-GERAN), 2.4m (94½in)

Fabric C (QVM1800-MILK), remnant for
strawberry stalk

Double-sided adhesive web, e.g. Vliesofix for
the appliqué

White sewing thread, e.g. Coats Cotton
number 50, colour 2716

Natural coloured embroidery yarn, e.g. Coats
Creative number 16, colour 1418

Seventeen small buttons in natural white

PATTERN SHEET A (WINE RED)

SEAM AND HEM ALLOWANCES
For all seams and edges 1cm (½in)
(already included).
See pattern sheet for small and large strawberries
with instructions on placement.

SEWING INSTRUCTIONS
Cut out all pieces and iron adhesive web on to the
appliqué fabric.
Transfer the large strawberry motif and stalk to
fabrics B and C and cut out without seam
allowances. Remove the backing paper from the
adhesive web, iron the motif on to the top side of
the quilt cover according to the placement
instructions (first the strawberry and then the
stalk on top).
Sew around the strawberry: select a stronger
sewing needle (90–100) and use the natural-
coloured embroidery yarn as a top thread. Check
the size of the stitch on a remnant of fabric, stitch
length approximately 3.5mm (¼in). If necessary,
relax the top thread tension a little. Sew roughly
over the shape of the strawberry and the stalk
two to three times with the natural-coloured
embroidery yarn; at the same time, sew over the
offset, transferred outlines of the stalk two to
three times. Sew on the buttons by hand as
indicated using embroidery thread.

Iron on the three small strawberries to the top
side of the pillowcase. Position 8cm (3¼in) from
the top to the top edge of the strawberries, with a

distance of 4cm (1½in) between the motifs.
Sew around the strawberries and embroider the
stalks by machine: transfer the outline of the stalks
on to the fabric as shown. Sew roughly around the
outlines of the offset strawberries twice, using the
natural-coloured embroidery yarn, at the same
time sewing the offset stalk once or twice. Change
the sewing needle and thread again.

Iron under the bottom edges of the bedding pieces
by 3cm (1¼in) to the wrong side, turn up a 1cm
(½in) seam allowance and sew in place 2cm (¾in)
from the edge.
Turn up the hemmed edge of fabric A by 20cm
(7¾in) right sides together. Iron the edge and fold
up again.
Sew together the pieces of the slip-on covers for
the bedding: place the quilt cover underside
(fabric B) right sides together with the quilt cover
top side (fabric A). The top edges line up exactly,
while the bottom edge of fabric A will stick out
20cm (7¾in) below fabric B. Fold the overlapping
edge at the ironed crease on to fabric B by 20cm
(7¾in). The right side of fabric A lies on top of the
wrong side of fabric B, with the sides flush with
one another. Tack the pieces together well. Stitch
the side seams and the top edge together. Neaten
the seam allowances together using zigzag stitch.
Proceed with the pillows in exactly the same way
as for the quilt cover. The hole for slipping in the
pillow is on the short side and uses the same
measurements as for the quilt cover.

		NOT ON THE PATTERN SHEET:		
PATTERN PIECES	1	Quilt cover top side	1.54m × 97cm (60¾in × 38¼in)	1 × fabric A
	2	Quilt cover underside	1.34m × 97cm (52¾in × 38¼in)	1 × fabric B
	3	Pillowcase top side	42cm × 84cm (16½in × 33in)	1 × fabric A
	4	Pillowcase underside	42cm × 64cm (16½in × 25¼in)	1 × fabric B

Children's bed linen with dolphins

LEVEL OF DIFFICULTY 2

SIZE
Quilt cover 1.3m × 95cm (51¼in × 37½in)
Pillows 40cm × 60cm (15¾in × 23½in) with reversible, slip-on pillowcases

MATERIALS
Fabric A (QVM1600-RAIN), 2m (78¾in)

Fabric B (QVM1800-RAIN), 2.45m (96½in)

Double-sided adhesive web, e.g. Vliesofix for the appliqué

White sewing thread, e.g. Coats Cotton number 50, colour 2716

Mercerised yarn, mid-blue

PATTERN SHEET B (DARK GREEN)

SEAM AND HEM ALLOWANCES
For all seams and edges 1cm (½in) (already included).
See pattern sheet for small and large dolphins with instructions on placement.

SEWING INSTRUCTIONS
Cut out all pieces according to the instructions and iron adhesive web on to the appliqué fabric before cutting out.
Transfer the dolphin motif to the piece of fabric and cut out without seam allowances. Remove the backing paper from the adhesive web, iron the dolphin on to the top side of the quilt cover according to the placement instructions. Embroider once around the dolphin with a narrow zigzag stitch. Sew around the shape of the dolphin by hand with mercerised yarn and decorate with simple tacking stitches. Embroider on the eye by hand, also using mercerised yarn. Draw on the small dolphin motif in the centre of the pillowcase on the top side according to the placement instructions and sew using tacking stitch.

If you do not like the look of the hand sewing, then use the traditional appliqué method or the method described for the strawberry bag on page 40.

Iron under the bottom edges of the bedding pieces by 3cm (1¼in) to the wrong side, turn up a 1cm (½in) seam allowance and sew in place 2cm (¾in) from the edge.
Turn up the hemmed edge of fabric A by 20cm (7¾in), right sides together. Iron the edge and fold up again.
Sew together the pieces of the slip-on covers for the quilt cover: place the quilt cover underside (fabric B) right sides together with the quilt cover top side (fabric A). The top edges line up exactly, while the bottom edge of fabric A will stick out 20cm (7¾in) below fabric B. Fold the overlapping edge at the ironed crease on to fabric B by 20cm (7¾in). The right side of fabric A lies on top of the wrong side of fabric B, with the sides flush with one another. Tack the pieces together well. Stitch the side seams and the top edge together. Neaten the seam allowances together using zigzag stitch. Proceed with the pillows in exactly the same way as for the quilt cover. The hole for slipping in the pillow is on the short side and uses the same measurements as for the quilt cover.

PATTERN PIECES	NOT ON THE PATTERN SHEET:		
1	Quilt cover top side	1.54m × 97cm (60¾in × 38¼in)	1 × fabric A
2	Quilt cover underside	1.34m × 97cm (52¾in × 38¼in)	1 × fabric B
3	Pillowcase top side	42cm × 84cm (16½in × 33in)	1 × fabric A
4	Pillowcase underside	42cm × 64cm (16½in × 25¼in)	1 × fabric B

Dreamy bed linen

LEVEL OF DIFFICULTY 3

SIZE
Quilt cover 1.4m × 2m
(55in × 78¾in)
Pillows 80cm × 80cm
(31½in × 31½in) with
linen zip fastenings

MATERIALS
Fabric A (QTW1800-RED),
3m (118in)

Fabric B (QTW2000-GREEN),
see diagram
for measurements

Fabric C (QVM1800-GERAN),
see diagram
for measurements

Fabric D (QTW2100-FOX),
1.5m (59in)

White sewing thread, e.g.
Coats Cotton number 50,
colour 2716

Zip fastener, 1.35m (53¼in),
e.g. bed linen Opti S40, item
1810, white, colour 09

Zip fastener, 76cm (30in),
e.g. bed linen Opti S40, item
1810, white, colour 004

PATTERN PIECES
See diagram.
Measurements do not include a seam allowance.

SEAM AND HEM ALLOWANCES
Fabric A: bottom edge of top side 2cm (¾in),
bottom edge of reverse side 3cm (1¼in).
For all other seams and edges 1cm (½in).

SEWING INSTRUCTIONS
Cut out all pieces according to the instructions.
Place the fabric strips for the top of the quilt
cover next to one another, right sides together,
tack and sew together. Neaten the seam
allowances together using zigzag stitch. Proceed
with the reverse in the same way.
Place the zip fastener along the bottom seam
edges of the top and bottom sides (lay zip
fastener right sides together with the zip
fastener edge flush with the raw edge and tack
in place).
Sew the long zip fastener 1cm (½in) from the
edge on both sides and neaten the seam
allowances using zigzag stitch. Lay the pieces
right sides together with the wrong side of the
top of the quilt cover fabric on top. Fold down
the edge of the zip fastener to the front and pin
in place. Sew the side seams and top edge.
Neaten the seam allowances together using
zigzag stitch (see instructions on page 110).
Turn the cover out, and iron the edges flat along
the hidden zip fastening.

The pillowcase is made in the same way as the
quilt cover.

Diagram for top side of quilt cover

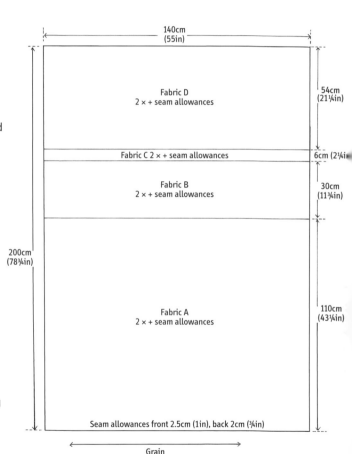

Delicate little bag

LEVEL OF DIFFICULTY 1

SIZE
30cm × 25cm (11¾in × 9in)

MATERIALS
Fabric A (QVM1300-MILK), see table
for measurements

Fabric B (QVM1800-OLIVE), see table
for measurements

Satin ribbon, 2cm (¾in) wide, 52cm (20½in)

Cord or ribbon, 1cm (½in) wide, 70cm (27½in)

Khaki sewing thread, e.g. Coats Cotton
number 50, colour 7323

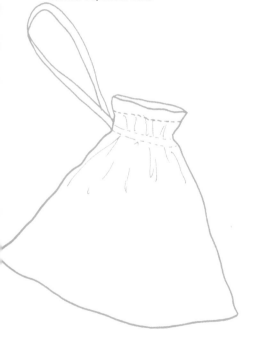

SEAM ALLOWANCES
1cm (½in) seam allowances included.

SEWING INSTRUCTIONS
Cut out all the pieces according to the
instructions. Sew one bag from both pieces: place
right sides together, tack and sew side and base
seams. Iron the seam allowances flat. Turn the
outer bag right side out. Fold the trim of the inner
bag towards the outside by 8cm (3¼in). Turn up a
1cm (½in) seam allowance, iron and tack.
Push the outer bag on to the inner bag with the
side seams meeting.
Place the seam allowance of the outer bag under
the trim of the inner bag. Sew satin ribbon to the
short sides, then fold in half lengthways and tack
on to the outer bag as a decorative braid beneath
the trim.

Sew a second seam for the drawstring channel 2cm
(¾in) from the edge of the trim.
Make an additional, small zigzag seam along the
side seam on both lockstitch seams, 2cm (¾in)
long, adjusting the stitch to be as narrow as for a
buttonhole. Finish this off well with straight stitch.
Undo the first layer of fabric of the side seam
between the zigzag bar tacks. Thread through the
cord or ribbon and sew together or tie.

	NOT ON THE PATTERN SHEET:		
1	Outer bag	25cm × 52cm (9¾in × 20½in)	1 × fabric A
2	Inner bag	39cm × 52cm (15¼in × 20½in)	1 × fabric B

PATTERN PIECES

Pyjama bottoms for women

SEAM AND HEM ALLOWANCES

For all seams and edges 1cm (½in).

SEWING INSTRUCTIONS

Cut out all the pieces according to the pattern. Neaten the side seams, inside leg seams and the crotch seams using zigzag stitch.

Sew the side seams and iron the seam allowances flat. Sew the borders, right sides together, to the bottom edges of the legs. Turn the borders down and iron the seam allowances into the borders. Sew the embroidery motif by machine: transfer the flower to the left leg according to the placement instructions. Select a stronger sewing needle (90–100) and use the red embroidery yarn as a top thread. Check the size of the stitch on a remnant of fabric, stitch length approximately 3.5mm (¼in). If necessary, relax the top thread tension a little. Sew roughly over the shape of the flower twice. Change to natural-coloured embroidery yarn and sew over the outlines, slightly offset, one to two times. Change the sewing needle and thread again. Sew the inside leg seams and iron the seam allowances flat.

Fold the borders in half towards the inside, turn up the seam allowances and tack in place just above the joining seam. Stitch the borders from the right side into the joining seam, so that they are just caught from the inside.

Pull the pyjama halves inside one another, right sides together, and sew the crotch seam in one go. Fold the waistband inside along the fold line at the top edge of the pyjamas, and turn up the seam allowances and tack in place. Sew 3cm (1¼in) away from the edge, leaving a 4cm (1½in) opening for the elastic. Work out the width of the elasticated waist and cut the elastic with a 6cm (2¼in) seam allowance and thread through. Sew the elastic together with a 3cm (1¼in) overlap by hand or by machine. Close up the hole.

Tack the satin ribbon in place along the top edge following the waistband seam. Sew on to the waistband seam 1.5cm (⅝in) from the centre front. Work out the length of the ties and shorten if necessary. Turn up the raw edges of the satin ribbon twice and finish by hand, tying into a bow. Sew the button by hand to the centre of the embroidered flower.

PATTERN PIECES AND MOTIFS		
1	Front pyjama piece	2 × fabric A
2	Back pyjama piece	2 × fabric A
3	Front hem border	2 × fabric B on the fold line
4	Embroidery flower with placement instructions	
	The waistband (3cm [1¼in]) for the elasticated waist	
	is cut and the fold line on the pattern is marked	

LEVEL OF DIFFICULTY 2

SIZE
8/10, 12/14, 16/18

MATERIALS
Fabric A (QVM1800-GERAN),
1.8m (70¾in) – 1.9m (74¾in)
– 2m (78¾in)

Fabric B (QVM1700-GRAPE),
20cm (7¾in)

Soft elastic, 2.5cm wide,
60cm (23½in) – 70cm
(27½in) – 80cm (31½in)

Washable satin ribbon, 1cm
(½in) wide, matching colour,
1.8m (70¾in)

Red sewing thread, e.g.
Coats Cotton number 50,
colour 7810

Red and natural-coloured
embroidery yarns, e.g. Coats
Creative number 16, colours
7810 and 1418

Decorative button for the
embroidered flower

PATTERN SHEET B
(LIGHT BLUE)

Pyjama bottoms for children

Pyjama bottoms
for children

STRAIGHT LEG,
NORMAL WIDTH

LEVEL OF DIFFICULTY 2

HEIGHT
98cm (38½in) – 1.1m (43¼in) – 1.22m (48in)

MATERIALS
Fabric A (QVM1600-RAIN), 90cm (35½in) –
1m (39¼in) – 1.1m (43¼in)

Fabric B (QVM1800-RAIN), remnant
30cm × 40cm (11¾in × 15¾in) for two pockets

Soft elastic, 2cm (¾in) wide, 60cm (23½in) –
65cm (25½in) – 70cm (27½in)

Fleece interfacing, remnant

Natural-coloured sewing thread, e.g. Coats
Cotton number 50, colour 1418

Piece of mercerised yarn, mid-blue, for
pocket motif

Cord, mid-blue, 80cm (31½in) – 90cm (35½in)
– 1m (39¼in)

Cord stoppers, matching colour

PATTERN SHEET B (LIGHT LILAC)

SEAM AND HEM ALLOWANCES

For all seams and edges 1cm (½in).
4cm (1½in) for pyjama hem.
The waistband (2.5cm [1in]) for the elasticated
waist is cut out and the fold line on the pattern
is marked.

SEWING INSTRUCTIONS

Cut out all the pieces according to the pattern.
Neaten the side seams, inside leg seams and the
crotch seams using zigzag stitch.
Sew the side seams and iron the seam
allowances flat.
Sew on the embroidered motif by hand: transfer
the dolphin motif to the left pocket and sew
around the shape by hand using a simple tacking
stitch or backstitch in mercerised yarn.
Iron under the seam allowances for the pockets to
the inside. Fold the pocket trims inside, turn up
the seam allowances and sew in place 4cm (1½in)
from the edge. Tack the pockets centred on the
side seams (17cm [6¾in] – 20cm [7¾in] – 23cm
[9in] from the top edge of the waistband) and sew
in place twice (1mm [⅛in] and 7mm [⅜in] from
the edge).

Sew the inside leg seams and iron the seam
allowances flat.
Pull the pyjama halves inside one another, right
sides together, and sew the crotch seam in one go.
Make the buttonholes (2cm [¾in] long) for the
drawstring channel in the pyjama waistband,
centred and 1.5cm (⅝in) from the front crotch
seam, having ironed on fleece interfacing to the
wrong side for reinforcement.
Fold the waistband inside along the fold line at
the top edge of the pyjamas, turn up the seam
allowances and tack in place. Sew 2.5cm (1in)
away from the edge, leaving a 4cm (1½in)
opening for the elastic. Work out the width of the
elasticated waist, cut the elastic with a 6cm
(2¼in) seam allowance and thread through. Sew
the elastic together by hand or by machine with a
3cm (1¼in) overlap. Close up the hole.
Thread through the cord, attach cord stoppers on
to the ends and knot.
Fold the seam allowances of the pyjama legs 4cm
(1½in) inside, turn up 1cm (½in) and sew in place
3cm (1¼in) from the edge of the hem.

PATTERN PIECES AND MOTIFS			
	1	Front pyjama piece	2 × fabric A
	2	Back pyjama piece	2 × fabric A
	3	Side pockets	2 × fabric B
	4	Embroidery motif of dolphin	

LEVEL OF DIFFICULTY 2

HEIGHT
1.46m (57½in) − 1.52m (59¾in) − 1.58m (62¼in)

MATERIALS
Fabric A (QVM1800-RAIN), 1.75m (69in) − 1.8m (70¾in) − 1.85m (72¾in)

Cotton waistband in khaki, 2cm (¾in) wide, 1.1m (43¼in)

Soft elastic, 1.5cm (½in) wide, 65cm (25½in) − 70cm (27½in) − 75cm (29½in)

Light blue sewing thread, e.g. Coats Cotton number 50, colour 2336

Sewing thread to match the ribbon around the leg hem, here Coats Cotton number 50, khaki, colour 7323

Khaki embroidery yarn, e.g. Coats Creative number 16, colour 7323

Small button for the eye of the embroidered shark

PATTERN SHEET B (LIGHT GREEN)

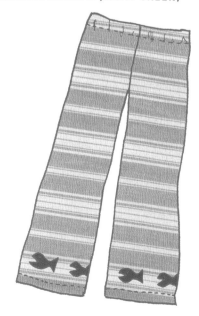

For all seams and edges 1cm (½in).
4cm (1½in) for pyjama hem.
The waistband (2cm [¾in]) for the elasticated waist is cut out and the fold line on the pattern is marked.

SEWING INSTRUCTIONS

Cut out all the pieces according to the pattern. Neaten the side seams, inside leg seams and the crotch seams using zigzag stitch.
Sew the side seams and iron the seam allowances flat.
Sew on the embroidered motif by machine. First transfer the shark motif to the left pyjama leg. Work out the position: here, the bottom edge of the shark is 13cm (5in) away from the bottom edge of the hem. The embroidery goes over the side seam, with the tail fin on the reverse of the pyjama leg. Select a stronger sewing needle (90–100) and use the khaki embroidery yarn as a top thread. Check the size of the stitch on a remnant of fabric, stitch length approximately 3.5mm (¼in). If necessary, relax the top thread tension a little.

Sew roughly over the shape of the shark two to three times and sew over with the embroidery yarn. Change the sewing needle and thread again. Sew the inside leg seams and iron the seam allowances flat.
Pull the pyjama halves inside one another, right sides together, and sew the crotch seam in one go. Fold the trim inside along the fold line at the top edge of the pyjamas, turn up the seam allowances and tack in place. Sew 2cm (¾in) away from the edge, leaving a 4cm (1½in) opening for the elastic. Work out the width of the elasticated waist, cut the elastic with a 6cm (2¼in) seam allowance and thread through. Sew the elastic together by hand or by machine with a 3cm (1¼in) overlap. Close up the hole.
Fold the seam allowances of the pyjama legs 4cm (1½in) inside, turn up 1cm (½in) and sew in place 3cm (1¼in) from the edge of the hem.
Measure the ribbon to fit, plus 2cm (¾in) extra and tack in place, so that the hem seam is concealed. Fold the end of the ribbon inside and sew the ribbon in place on either side. Sew on the button for the shark's eye by hand.

1	Front pyjama piece	2 × fabric A
2	Back pyjama piece	2 × fabric A
3	Embroidery motif of shark	

Pyjama bottoms for girls

NARROW LEG WITH SLIGHT FLARE AND DRAWSTRING ANKLE

LEVEL OF DIFFICULTY 2

HEIGHT
1.28m (50½in) – 1.4m (55in) – 1.52m (59¾in)

MATERIALS
Fabric A (QVM1600-GRAPE), 1m (39¼in) – 1.1m (43¼in) – 1.2m (47¼in)

Fabric B (QVM1800-GRAPE), 15cm (6in)

Soft elastic, 3.5cm (1½in) wide, 65cm (25½in) – 70cm (27½in) – 75cm (29½in)

Washable satin ribbon, 1cm (½in) wide, matching colour, 2m (79in) (1m [39½in] for waistband, 50cm [19¾in] each for drawstrings around the pyjama legs)

Fleece interfacing, remnant

Natural-coloured sewing thread, e.g. Coats Cotton number 50, colour 1418

Two decorative roses

PATTERN SHEET B (RED)

For all seams and edges 1cm (½in).
3cm (1¼in) for pyjama hem.

SEWING INSTRUCTIONS
Cut out all the pieces according to the pattern. Neaten the side seams, inside leg seams and the crotch seams using zigzag stitch.
Sew the side seams and iron the seam allowances flat.
Fold the seam allowances of the pyjama legs 3cm (1¼in) inside at the side seam, turn up 1cm (½in) and sew along for 3cm (1¼in) (1.5cm [⅝in] from the left and right of each side seam).

Iron under the seam allowances all around to the reverse side for the drawstring channels and sew the bottom edge following the width of the sewing machine foot. Tack the drawstring channels 2mm (⅛in) from the hem edge inside the pyjama leg centred on the side seams and sew round using a narrow stitch. Sew the dividing seam for the drawstring channels from the right side into the side seam to 1.5cm (⅝in) from the ends of the channel. Sew the inside leg seams and iron the seam allowances flat.

Pull the pyjama halves inside one another, right sides together, and sew the crotch seam in one go. Fold the seam allowances for the pyjama legs inside by 3cm (1¼in), turn up by 1cm (½in) and sew in place, leaving the drawstring channel free. Pull 50cm (19¾in) of satin ribbon through each one in a u-shape and tie at the bottom in a bow. Make the buttonholes for the drawstring channel in the pyjama waistband according to the pattern diagram and iron the fleece interfacing on to the wrong side to reinforce. Neaten the seam allowances along the short edges using zigzag stitch, then sew together right sides facing. Iron the seam allowances flat.

Sew the waistband to the pyjamas, right sides together, matching the waistband seam with the rear crotch seam and making sure that the buttonholes are centred at the front crotch seam. Iron the seam allowances into the pyjama waistband. Fold the pyjama waistband inside at the fold line, turn up the seam allowance and tack in place. Sew from the right side, leaving a 4cm (1½in) opening for the elastic. Work out the width of the elasticated waist, cut the elastic with a 6cm (2¼in) seam allowance and thread through. Sew the elastic together by hand or by machine overlapping by 3cm (1¼in). Close up the opening. Pull the satin ribbon through the buttonholes. Turn up the raw edges of the satin ribbon twice and close up by hand. Sew on little decorative roses to the side seam at the ends of the drawstring channel by hand.

If you make additional drawstring channels on the seams for the inside legs, the pyjamas can be gathered up, altering the length of the pyjamas by up to 10cm (4in).

NARROW LEG WITH SLIGHT FLARE AND DRAWSTRING ANKLE

1	Front pyjama piece	2 × fabric A
2	Back pyjama piece	2 × fabric A
3	Waistband, sewn on	1 × fabric B on the fold line
4	Drawstring channel, pyjama leg	2 × fabric B

STRAIGHT LEG, NORMAL WIDTH

1	Front pyjama piece	2 × fabric A
2	Back pyjama piece	2 × fabric A
3	Borders, pyjama hem	2 × fabric B on the fold line

STRAIGHT LEG, NORMAL WIDTH

LEVEL OF DIFFICULTY 2

HEIGHT
1.1m (43¼in) – 1.22m (48in) – 1.34m (52¾in)

MATERIALS
Fabric A (QVM1300-MILK), 1m (39¼in) – 1.1m (43¼in) – 1.2m (47¼in)

Fabric B (QVM1800-MILK), 15cm (6in)

Soft elastic, 3.5cm (1½in) wide, 60cm (23½in) – 65cm (25½in) – 70cm (27½in)

Satin ribbon, washable, 1cm (½in) wide, matching colour, 1.6m (63in)

Natural-coloured sewing thread, e.g. Coats Cotton number 50, colour 1418

Two decorative roses

PATTERN SHEET B (DARK BLUE)

SEAM AND HEM ALLOWANCES
For all seams and edges 1cm (½in).
The waistband (5cm [2in]) for the elasticated waist is cut out and the fold line on the pattern is marked.

SEWING INSTRUCTIONS

Cut out all the pieces according to the pattern. Neaten the side seams, inside leg seams and the crotch seams using zigzag stitch.

Sew the side seams and iron the seam allowances flat. Sew the borders to the bottom edges of the pyjama legs, right sides together. Turn the borders down and iron the seam allowances into the borders.

Sew the inside leg seams and iron the seam allowances flat.

Fold the borders in half towards the inside, turn up the seam allowances and tack in place just above the joining seam. Sew the borders from the right side into the joining seam, so that they are just caught from the inside.

Pull the pyjama halves inside one another, right sides together, and sew the crotch seam in one go. Fold the waistband at the top edge of the pyjamas inwards along the fold line, turn up the seam allowances and tack in place. Sew 5cm (2in) from the edge, leaving a 4cm (1½in) opening for the elastic. Work out the width of the elasticated waist, cut the elastic with a 6cm (2¼in) seam allowance and thread through. Sew the elastic together by hand or by machine, overlapping by 3cm (1¼in). Close up the opening.

Pyjama bottoms for men

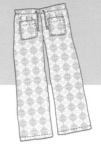

LEVEL OF DIFFICULTY 2

SIZE
38 – 40 – 42

MATERIALS
Fabric A (QVM1800-OLIVE), 2.3m (90½in) – 2.35m (92½in) – 2.4m (94½in)

Fabric B (QVM1700-VERBE), remnant for pocket

Soft elastic, 2.5cm (1in) wide, 85cm (33½in) – 90cm (35½in) – 95cm (37½in)

Washable satin ribbon, 5mm (¼in) wide, matching colour, 1.2m (47¼in)

Khaki sewing thread, e.g. Coats Cotton number 50, colour 7323

PATTERN SHEET B (BROWN)

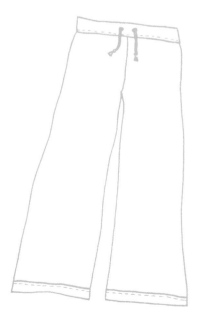

SEAM AND HEM ALLOWANCES
For all seams and edges 1cm (½in).
4cm (1½in) for pyjama hem (show hem allowance at the side).
4.5cm (1¾in) for pyjama waistband (show hem allowance at the side).
The waistband (3.5cm [1½in]) for the elasticated waist must also be included in the cut.

SEWING INSTRUCTIONS
Cut out all the pieces according to the pattern. Neaten the side seams, inside leg seams and the crotch seams using zigzag stitch.
Iron under to the inside the seam allowances for the rear pocket. Stitch the trim along the top edge of the pocket, fold inside, turn up the seam allowance and sew in place 2cm (¾in) from the edge, either incorporating the centred satin ribbon (14cm [5½in]) at the same time, or sew it later on to the lockstitch seam. Tack the rear pocket on to the left back pyjama piece following the placement instructions on the pattern and sew in place twice (1mm [⅛in] and 7mm [⅜in] from the edge).

Sew the side seams and iron the seam allowances flat.
Sew the inside leg seams and iron the seam allowances flat.
Pull the pyjama halves inside one another, right sides together, and sew the crotch seam in one go. Fold the waistband and the seam allowance (4.5cm [1¾in]) inside along the fold line at the top edge of the pyjamas, turn up the seam allowances and tack in place. Sew 3.5cm (1½in) away from the edge, leaving a 4cm (1½in) opening for the elastic. Work out the width of the elasticated waist, cut the elastic with a 6cm (2¼in) seam allowance and thread through. Sew the elastic together with a 3cm (1¼in) overlap by hand or by machine. Close up the hole.
Fold the seam allowances for the pyjama legs inside by 4cm (1½in), turn up 1cm (½in) and sew in place 3cm (1¼in) from the edge of the hem. Measure the satin ribbon accordingly with a 2cm (¾in) seam allowance and tack in place, so that the hem seam is concealed. Fold in the end of the ribbon and sew the ribbon centred in place.

PATTERN PIECES			
	1	Front pyjama piece	2 × fabric A
	2	Back pyjama piece	2 × fabric A
	3	Rear pocket	1 × fabric A
	4	Waistband for top edge of pyjamas	1 × fabric A (Cut 1.06m [41¾in] – 1.11m [43¾in] – 1.16m [45¾in] × 6cm [2¼in])
		NOT ON THE PATTERN SHEET:	
		Trim for rear pocket	2 × fabric B (2cm [¾in] × pocket width)

TOY TOWN

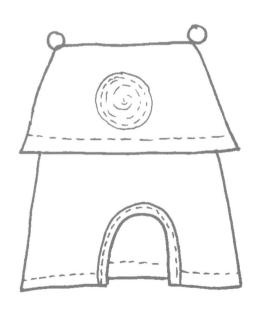

Play houses

SIZE

Tower house approximately 40cm (15¾in) high, base approximately 12cm (4¾in) diameter

Rose house approximately 20cm (7¾in) high, base approximately 16cm (6¼in) diameter

Striped house approximately 23cm (9in) high, base approximately 17cm × 17cm (6¾in × 6¾in)

MATERIALS

Various remnants of fabric, for size see pattern sheet

Volume fleece, single-sided, iron-on

Firm fleece interfacing

Corset tape, 1.5cm (⅝in) wide

Velvet ribbon, satin ribbon and mercerised yarn in matching colours

Buttons, beads, felt balls, silk roses, tiny bells

White sewing thread, e.g. Coats Cotton number 50, colour 2716 or other matching shade

PATTERN SHEET B (TOWER HOUSE TURQUOISE, ROSE HOUSE GREY, STRIPED HOUSE BURGUNDY)

SEAM AND HEM ALLOWANCES

For all seams and edges 1cm (½in).
Iron-on fleece interfacing with seam allowance, volume fleece without seam allowance.

SEWING INSTRUCTIONS

All the houses are sewn following the same procedure: cut out all the pattern pieces according to the pattern and the instructions above.
The outer fabric A is always reinforced, including the seam allowances, with firm fleece interfacing. The inner fabric B is always reinforced with volume fleece, omitting the seam allowances. The pieces are initially made individually and then stitched together. To make the round pieces more stable, corset tape can be incorporated into the seam allowances. The openings for turning or the open seams can be closed by hand or trimmed with ribbon. The decorations and seams are sewn up or stitched on at the very end.

One exception is the tiling structure on the roof of the tower, which is stitched on before it is sewn together.

Tower house

Sew together the side seam for tower A, right sides together. Iron the seam allowances flat and turn out.
Sew together tower B in the same way, but do not turn out.
Put tower B right sides together with tower A and sew along the bottom edge with the door opening. Pull tower B into tower A and iron the fold line edges neatly on top of one another.
Measure out the corset tape for the bottom edge (omitting the door opening). Place between the two fabrics, entering from the top, following around the bottom edge and tack in place from the right side.
Sew from the right side directly over the corset tape and 5mm (¼in) around the arch of the door.

PATTERN PIECES			
		TOWER HOUSE	
	1	Tower	1 × fabric A on the fold line
			1 × fabric B on the fold line
	2	Tower roof	1 × fabric A, 1 × fabric B
		ROSE HOUSE	
	1	House	1 × fabric A on the fold line
			1 × fabric B on the fold line
	2	House roof	1 × fabric A, 1 × fabric B
		STRIPED HOUSE	
	1	House wall	4 × fabric A (1 × omitting the door opening)
			4 × fabric B (1 × omitting the door opening)
	2	Roof part 1	1 × fabric A on the fold line
			1 × fabric B on the fold line
	3	Roof part 2	2 × fabric A, 2 × fabric B

The corset tape can also be sewn in place with another seam or a decorative stitch. Turn up the seam allowances for the top edge of both pieces and iron.

Measure the corset tape and tack into the folded-in seam allowance for tower A.

Tack the top edges neatly on top of one another. Sew the tower pieces together close to the edge and then 7mm (⅜in) away from the edge (or perhaps with a decorative stitch), incorporating the corset tape at the same time.

Sew a little rose over the door opening.

TOWER HOUSE ROOF

Stitch the roof tiling structure on to tower roof A. For a subtle look, choose a matching yarn; if you want the lockstitch seams to stand out more, use thicker sewing thread (e.g. Coats Creative number 16 embroidery thread) and a contrasting colour.

Place the side seam for tower roof A right sides together, tack and sew together from bottom to top. Iron the seam flat and turn the piece right side out. Sew tower roof B together in the same way, but do not turn out. Iron the seam allowances for both roof pieces to the wrong side. Measure the length of corset tape and tack into the folded-in seam allowance for roof A.

Put roof A into roof B and tack the bottom edges neatly on top of one another. Sew together close to the edge and at 7mm (⅜in) from the edge, incorporating the corset tape.

Decorate the roof with beads and a little rose on the tip. Turn the roof inside out and sew a tiny bell to the inside tip of the roof.

Rose house

Follow the instructions for the tower house. The door opening is decorated with a scrap of velvet ribbon and the top edge trimmed with satin bias binding. A mother-of-pearl button is sewn above the door.

ROSE HOUSE ROOF

Follow the instructions for the tower roof. The roof is not reinforced with corset tape; the wide base makes it sufficiently sturdy. The bottom hem edge is not turned up, but trimmed with a piece of tape cut from a remnant of fabric and decorated with a wavy embroidery stitch. The tip of the roof is also decorated with a mother-of-pearl button.

Striped house

First, sew together all four side pieces for house A and also for house B, right sides together. Iron the seam allowances flat. Corset tape is not required; continue working as for the tower house or the rose house. The corners of the house can be made more stable by topstitching a short distance from the edge from the right side. The door arch is decorated here with satin bias binding.

STRIPED HOUSE ROOF

First, sew the side pieces right sides together into roof piece 1. For best results, sew the seams from bottom to top.
Corset tape is not required; continue working as for the tower house. The roof is decorated inside and out with an appliqué and with felt bobbles.

The houses are washable and can be laid together flat and carried around, making them suitable for small children too.
Please be especially careful to avoid sewing on tiny pieces that could be swallowed by very young children. Instead, you could sew crackle foil or little bells in between the shapes.

BASIC TECHNIQUES AND TIPS

Accessories

The correct sewing tools will make your life easier and will achieve good results.

The following materials and tools are needed as a basic requirement for all projects: tailor's tape measure, good dressmaking scissors, small scissors for snipping sewing threads, tissue paper, photocopy paper and tracing wheel, tailor's chalk or marker pen for fine markings, stitch unpicker, pins, tacking thread, hand-sewing needles, paper scissors, pencil, felt-tip pen and, for many projects, a ruler and a pair of compasses.

When transferring patterns, a flexible curve template or a tailor's square is also useful. Retailers stock a wide range of sewing machines in various price ranges. If you do not yet have a sewing machine and would like to invest in one, do not necessarily buy the cheapest. We recommend that you seek advice from a specialist retailer. It is best to use an iron with a steam function, as this will be able to iron thicker fabrics and those susceptible to creasing, such as denim or linen. You will also need an ironing board and possibly a sleeve board too. Heat-sensitive fabrics can be covered with an ironing cloth to prevent shine. It can also be used to protect the ironing board from traces of adhesive when ironing on fleece interfacing.

Preparation

As most fabrics run when first washed, we recommend that you wash them before cutting out. Use the recommended wash programme and iron the fabric flat again before cutting. Prewashing is especially important for clothing, hats and pieces that have a lot of interfacing or a zip fastener that will not shrink in the same way, leaving unsightly creases.

All materials used must also be washable, especially satin and velvet ribbons, buttons, beads and decorations. Simply remove karabiner hooks or clasps before washing.

Quantity of fabric

The quantity of fabric stated refers to the original fabric from the Free Spirit Collection. All fabrics are made from pure cotton and are 1.15m (45¼in) wide. The measurements given in the book are for prewashed fabrics. When purchasing, approximately five per cent must therefore be added. For fabrics with large patterns, particular care must be taken with the pattern run. With these designs, the greater quantity needed has already been incorporated into the measurements.

Combining the fabrics

There are countless ways in which fabrics can be uniquely combined according to your own imagination, ideas and requirements. Here are a few good tips for the inexperienced.
Ensure a balanced mix – a striking, large or multi-coloured pattern (e.g. large flowers) always works better if it is combined with a quiet, plain or small, all-over pattern (stripes, checks or dots) and not when it is competing with another dominant design.
It works well if the fabrics have something in common, such as a repeated colour, a motif or a common style.
Place the fabrics next to each other before cutting out and experiment with various combinations. Special care must be taken with designs with a high white content to ensure that the shades of white match: natural white does not always go well with brilliant white and can often look dirty in comparison.

Cutting out

Trace the pattern pieces and all the markings from the pattern sheet on to tissue paper using a pencil or felt-tip pen and set-square/curve template. Cut out the pattern and pin on to the reverse of the fabric. Pay attention to the grain of the fabric. Draw on the indicated seam allowance using chalk or a marker pen and cut out. Before removing the tissue paper from the fabric, mark all the outlines and seam lines, as well as the important markings such as darts, buttonholes and joining lines, using tailor's chalk or a marker pen.

Trace templates on to tissue paper for appliqués or embroidery and, using a tracing wheel and photocopying paper, transfer to the right side of the fabric. Trace the outlines of the motifs with non-permanent marker pen or tailor's chalk.

If appliqués are to be covered with double-sided adhesive interfacing, the motif can also be drawn in reverse on the backing paper side of the interfacing. Cut out the interfacing generously and iron on to the reverse side. Cut along the outlines drawn, remove the backing paper and iron on the appliqué.

Ironing and tacking

Even if these steps sometimes appear tiresome, they are still worth the effort. A neatly ironed flat seam can be made a lot more easily by following the steps below, avoiding creases and inaccuracies. Wherever possible, iron the seams from the wrong side to prevent any shine.
An ironing cloth will protect the iron from traces of adhesive from interfacing fabrics.
For straight and simple seams, you can use pins. Always place the pins at right angles to the seam, which will hold the fabrics together better and the pins will not get caught in the machine; you can also remove them more easily whilst sewing. Complicated seams, rounded edges, zip fasteners and ribbons are best tacked on by hand using tacking thread and will be more secure. Experienced dressmakers can, of course, use pins here too.

Darts in the base

In order to give a bag volume at the base or a base to stand on, darts can be sewn from the reverse side: place the corners at the base of the bag in such a way that the side seam runs along the centre of the base in the direction of the tips of the corners. Sew the darts at right angles to the side seam at the stated distance from the tip of the corner. The greater the distance, the deeper the base. The height of the bag will reduce due to the base darts in proportion to the newly gained depth of the base.

For a box pleat, first mark both side lines as well as the centre of the fold. Fold the fabric from the right side along the side lines and iron. Place the ironed sides in the direction of the centre of the fold, so that the side lines meet. Tack the fold inside the seam allowance or as indicated.

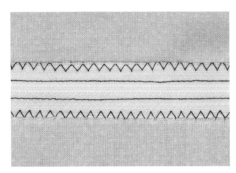

Place both sides of the zip fastener over the fabric, right sides together and flush with the raw edges. Tack in place and sew 1cm (½in) from the edge on both sides. Neaten the seam allowances using zigzag stitch.

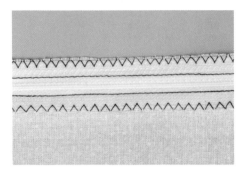

Place the pieces right sides together with the reverse side of the fabric of the front piece on top. Fold down the edge of the zip fastener to the front and pin in place.

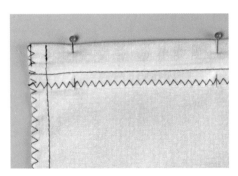

Sew the side seams and the open edge. Neaten the seam allowances together using zigzag stitch.

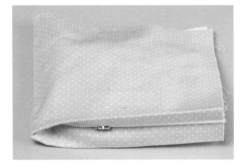

Turn out the cover and iron the edges neatly on top of one another along the concealed zip fastener.

Gathering threads/
gathering up fabric

Appliqués and embroidered
motifs

Filling with polyester
granules

In order to be able to sew on gathered fabric, you need to gather it up with the help of gathering threads.

These threads are sewn in two rows approximately 7mm (⅜in) and 1cm (½in) from the edge, either sewn by hand using stitches approximately 5mm (¼in) long or sewn by machine. For the latter, select the largest stitch length, relax the tension slightly and leave approximately 10cm (4in) of thread over at each end. Do not secure the stitching with bar tacks. Gather up the fabric to the required width, tie the ends of the gathering threads securely at the start and the finish or secure with stitches. Space the fabric folds evenly. Place the gathered fabric right sides together on to the corresponding piece and tack in place, making sure again that the fabric folds are evenly spaced. Sew the gathers in place, remove the gathering threads and, if necessary, neaten the seam allowances together using zigzag stitch.

The appliqué technique in this book differs from the traditional method in that some imprecision and some fraying of the edges is intended as part of the desired effect. Sewing several times around the edge of the appliqué with embroidery yarn enables freer work, with the embroidered seams overlapping from time to time and even deviating from the outline. A test piece is always helpful if you do not feel confident enough to work straight on the final piece. The motifs can of course also be sewn using the well-tried appliqué method, and embroidery motifs can be complemented by hand using mercerised yarn. Experiment with whichever method suits you the best.

Polyester granules are very light and are good to use as a filling, especially as they are so malleable. They are particularly suitable as a filling for large cushions.

As they are not washable, the little styropor balls should be put inside an inner cushion that is closed up using lockstitch.

The inner cushion can be made from light cotton fabric, linen or other thickly woven cotton. An old cushion cover could also be used.

Cut out the pattern pieces for the corresponding cushion cover (quite a bit larger), allowing at least 10cm (4in) on each side. Sew together the seams for the pattern pieces, leaving an opening of approximately 30cm (11¾in) for filling.

Fill the inner cushion with polyester granules and temporarily close up the opening to see whether you have enough filling. It is advisable to fill it more firmly than usual, as the filling will become looser with use. Finally, close up the opening for filling using lockstitch.

If you are planning several projects using filling granules, it is advisable to do all the filling at the same time and get someone to help you. The little balls can escape easily and it is simpler if someone holds apart the opening for filling and the other person does the filling.

First published in Great Britain 2010 by Search Press Limited,
Wellwood, North Farm Road, Tunbridge Wells, Kent TN2 3DR

Original German edition published as Design Buch Nähen.

Copyright © 2009 frechverlag GmbH, Stuttgart, Germany (www.frech.de)

This edition published by arrangement with Claudia Böhme Rights & Literary Agency, Hannover, Germany (www.agency-boehme.com)

English translation by Cicero Translations

English edition edited and typeset by GreenGate Publishing Services

ISBN: 978-1-84448-604-5

Layout: Petra Theilfarth

Photos: frechverlag GmbH, 70499 Stuttgart; lichtblick GmbH, Jochen Frank, Laichingen; lichtpunkt, Michael Ruder, Stuttgart (photos of all the individual steps)

We would like to thank the following companies for their support with this book:

Coats GmbH, 79341 Kenzingen
www.coatsgmbh.com

GreenGate Interiors, DK-2930 Klampenborg
www.greengate.dk

Rayher Hobby GmbH, 88471 Laupheim
www.rayher-hobby.de

THANK YOU! also to: Tobi, Tim, Lilja, Lilly, Adrian, Amelie, Ida, Paulus, Susi, Eva, Katri, Jussi, Miri, Susanne, Waltraud, Karl, Rudolf and Marjatta

Suppliers

All of the fabrics used in this book are from the Free Spirit Collection and are widely available worldwide. For information on suppliers, please visit the website: www.freespiritfabric.com

Although all of the designs used in this book are currently available, the Publishers cannot guarantee that this will always be the case. If you have difficulty in obtaining any of the fabric mentioned, then any good quality, cotton fabrics can be used instead.

Printed in China.